Richard Frazer was minister of C
from 2003 to his retirement in 2(
winning Grassmarket Communit
sanctuary and support to people dealing with multiple complex
issues. He has also been influential in the revival of pilgrimage
in Scotland and in the Church of Scotland's decision officially
to promote and revive pilgrimage after 450 years.

Praise for *Travels with a Stick*

'Richard's pilgrimage, fittingly, reads as a parable: unable to walk through injury, he heals and carries on, exhausted but resolute. His lengthy wandering, carrying only what can be borne, reveals the luxury of privation, and the breath-step of a long meditation underlines the importance of the journey, not the goal, on our present-day Pilgrim's Progress. It is an absolute delight walking the Camino with Richard'

Greg Wise

'An honest appraisal of life, belief and a poignant reminder that journeying with all kinds of people is often the best thing we ever get the chance to do'

Ricky Ross

'In the midst of his vulnerability and self-proclaimed vigour, Frazer reveals, in beautiful prose, the freedom and trust that the Camino brings: communities of faith and friendship'

Church Times

'Remarkable in both honesty and gratitude. A powerful account of how expectations and ambitions can be reframed and changed by the world-famous pilgrimage to allow deeper insights and lessons to emerge'

Life and Work

'Friendly and candid, Frazer recounts his journey with all its ups and downs, detailing the breathtaking scenery of his surroundings and the fascinating people he meets along the way . . . An inspiring read and a journey well worth taking with Frazer as your well-versed tour guide'

The Courier

TRAVELS WITH A STICK

A PILGRIM'S JOURNEY TO
SANTIAGO DE COMPOSTELA

RICHARD FRAZER

BIRLINN

For Kate, Will, Jean and Tom — joyful companions

This edition first published in 2025 by
Birlinn Limited
West Newington House
10 Newington Road
Edinburgh
EH9 1QS

Copyright © Richard Frazer 2019, 2025

Foreword copyright © Alastair McIntosh, 2019
Map drawn by Pixo Creative Services

ISBN 978 1 78027 929 9

The right of Richard Frazer to be identified as Author of this work
has been asserted by him in accordance with the Copyright,
Designs and Patents Act 1988.

All rights reserved. No part of this publication may be reproduced in any
form or by any means without permission from the publisher.
British Library Cataloguing in Publication Data

A catalogue record for this book is available from the British Library.

Designed by James Hutcheson
Typeset by Initial Typesetting Services, Edinburgh

Papers used by Birlinn Ltd are from well-managed forests
and other responsible sources

Printed and bound by Clays Ltd, Elcograf S.p.A.

CONTENTS

	List of Illustrations	vii
	Map	viii
	Introduction to the 2025 Edition	xi
	Foreword	xvii
	Prologue: Meeting St Jacques	1
1	Setting Off	15
2	Le Puy-en-Velay	22
3	The Beast of Gévaudan	31
4	The Kindness of Strangers	43
5	Get Thee to a Nunnery	49
6	The Rule of Resonance	53
7	Bread-sharer for the Journey	59
8	Journey to Middle-earth	64
9	The Coupar Angus of France	68
10	The Interior Pilgrimage	73
11	Last Day in France	77
12	Into Spain	82
13	A Pilgrim Community	91
14	The Human Torch	98
15	The Pilgrim's Tale	106
16	Unexpected Encounter	124
17	Chicken in the Church	136
18	Mind-numbing Meseta	146

19	Deviation to Santander	158
20	Poisoned Food – Poisoned Relationships?	167
21	Into the Mountains	180
22	Santiago, Mata Moros	195
23	Nearing Santiago	202

Acknowledgements   217
Bibliography   219

LIST OF ILLUSTRATIONS

St Jacques in the cathedral of Le Puy-en-Velay
Descending into Monistrol-d'Allier
Dinner in Le Domaine du Sauvage
Estaing
With the stick in Conques
Heading out of Conques
Jon and me
Roncesvalles
Looking towards La Rioja
Puente la Reina
Shadows of evening after a long day on the way to Los Arcos
The king and queen ready to bop at Cirauqui
Wine on tap
Free dinner at Villa Franca
A *cruciero*
Myron and Jacques take a breather
Ancient Roman road
The cathedral of Burgos
With Santo Domingo
Jo and me taking in the aroma of Galicia
Proof that the starting point of the Camino, like any pilgrimage, is wherever you want it to be
The Benedictine monastery at Samos
Journey's end: at Santiago de Compostela
My completed pilgrim passport

The Camino
to Santiago de Compostela

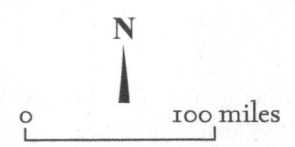

N

0 — 100 miles

Bay of Biscay

Santiago de Compostela
'An ending or a beginning?'

'The Feast Day of St Francis'
O Cebreiro

SANTANDER

Saint-Jean Pied-de-Port

Los Arcos
'Wine on Tap'

Roncesv...
Pamplon...

Samos
'An uncomfortable experience with Santiago, Mata Moros. My friend Jo arrives.'

León

Santo Domingo

La Meseta
'Mind-numbing terrain'

Burgos

La Rioja

Ven...
'Where I came across extraordinary road-side sh...'

'Meeting Eugenia, who was guided onto the right path by crows'

'Walking with my wife, Kate, and learning about Santo Domingo, architect of the Camino'

PORTUGAL

•MADRID

SPAIN

FRANCE

Le Puy-en-Velay
'Thoughts about Robert Louis Stevenson (Travels with a Donkey) and the Knights Templar, guardians of the Pilgrim Way'

Aumont-Aubrac
'Disaster with my feet, and meeting St Jacques'

Livinhac-le-Haut
'The Coupar Angus of France'

Figeac
'An empty head makes space for reflection'

Conques
'Cathedral in the woods'

St-Pierre-de-Bessuéjouls
'True hospitality from Francoise & Gilles. My friend Jon arrives – a companion for part of the way'

Massip
'Lessons in gratitude from a gentle woman'

MARSEILLE

'...oss the Pyrenees and into Spain'

Pyrenees

'...aking a new friend he shared his story'

BARCELONA

Mediterranean Sea

INTRODUCTION TO THE 2025 EDITION

'I went out for a walk and realised that going out was really a going in.' These words of John Muir have echoed in my mind ever since I first read them. My Camino experience and every other pilgrimage journey before and since has gone on transforming the grain of my thinking – about faith, about life and about the Church I served as a minister from 1986, when I was ordained, until I stepped back from full-time ministry at the end of 2023.

It is impossible to underestimate the extent to which the Christian faith has shaped the Western world, but the Church in almost all its manifestations has been on the retreat for several generations. The irony is that coincidentally with the dramatic shift away from conventional church going, people have set off on their own spiritual search, many choosing the ancient habit of pilgrimage to find the spiritual nourishment they still crave.

When we are uncertain, confused and are not sure what is next, many of us will set out for a walk to clear our heads. Two of Jesus's disciples did just that when, on the first Easter Sunday, following the judicial murder of their leader, they set out for a walk to Emmaus. (Luke 24: 13–35). They meet a stranger on the road, and their hearts 'burn within them' as they talk and walk together. They come to realise that the message of Jesus has not died with him but lives on within them.

The demise of western Christianity, hastened by the impact of the Covid 19 pandemic, is a form of cultural devastation. However, whether part of a faith community or not, through pilgrimage and other means (outside of the Church), people seem to be discovering that whilst the old institutional order of things might be breaking down, the Spirit is alive and well.

On a pilgrimage, people may encounter the Spirit unexpectedly, in a visceral way, rather than through a scheduled set of practices. One of the criticisms of conventional Christianity today is that it gives us a lot of information about the Divine nature but rarely enables us to encounter the Divine in the startling way that a pilgrimage can. The first question asked at the first book talk I gave in 2019 came from a man who described himself as a life-long atheist. He began: 'Something happened to me on that journey, and I am going to have to spend the rest of my life trying to work out what that was.'

It was in 2012 that I walked the Camino de Santiago, and it was busy then. Now, after the pandemic and in the midst of so much uncertainty in the world, the appetite for pilgrim journeys seems only to grow. Religious institutions may be struggling to stay afloat, and people also see so much else of what was dependable in the world unravelling. The Climate Emergency calls into question the global industrial economy that emerged in the Christian west. Current tensions weigh heavily on people throughout the world, and many are searching for ways which will transform relationships between peoples, challenge poverty and injustice and promote a fairer deal for people and the planet.

I continue to walk pilgrim ways whenever time allows, and since stepping back from full-time ministry, I have begun to lead pilgrim journeys, exploring the meaning of faith with others; people from churches and people without faith, but all with enquiring minds and questions, all searching for the wisdom for human and planetary flourishing.

I have kept in touch with a number of my fellow pilgrims from 2012 who continue to be inspired by their journey. Myron returned to his community café with renewed energy and belief in the path he had chosen, offering a forward-looking vision for what a church community could look like through offering hospitality, inclusivity and an unconditional welcome to all in his community. Neve continues to nurture and home educate her seven children, and, as part of that education, has returned to the Camino with them all. When sharing her thoughts on pilgrimage with us on a visit to Scotland, she said, 'Along the way we meet such a diverse collection of people. We need to learn that difference enriches our lives more than threatening them.' What better lesson for her children, and us all, to learn?

A practice once outlawed by the Reformed Church is now drawing huge numbers to walk pilgrimage routes and explore the narrative of faith. There are now close to 2,000 miles of designated pilgrim walks in Scotland alone, from the St Magnus Way in Orkney to the Whithorn Pilgrim Way in the south-west.

In the Church of Scotland, the response to the decline of the institution has been largely a bureaucratic one, governed by numbers and money. At times there seems little vision around about what the Church must do to reimagine its role as a source of transformative encounter with the Spirit at the heart of life. It is not an effective strategy simply to try to recruit new members and restore our fortunes by streamlining existing structures.

The Biblical account of the period after Jesus's death suggests that resurrection is not the same thing as restoration. At first, those who were a part of Jesus's inner circle dismissed the women who declared he was risen by suggesting these were 'idle tales' (Luke 24: 11). It took a while for people to realise that the death of Jesus was the prelude to another future. It would be different, but the message and the Spirit behind the message was not finished by the events of Good Friday. The challenging road of transformation began on that pilgrimage walk to Emmaus.

Pilgrimage has taught me that there is no going back to restore what has been. Life and faith are journeys that look forward and face in one direction. We certainly learn from the past, and, as we travel through the landscape, stories we read on these journeys unfold to us a rich and illuminating narrative of faith and spirituality going back many centuries that can help to underwrite another future.

Western society, along with the Church, struggles to make sense of a world utterly transformed by industrialisation, global warfare, post-industrial decline, globalisation and the arrival of new technologies that were inconceivable in their reach, power, influence and control even twenty years ago. But there is no going back, and, like pilgrims, we go forward in the adventure of spiritual discovery. The challenge for our churches is a humbling one. It is to discover where the Spirit is thriving and learn how to adapt to a world utterly transformed in a few generations so that they might continue to be a catalyst for spiritual nourishment for all.

More than ever, in this period of great unsettlement, the practice of pilgrimage is treading a path in which we can reimagine the world. As we follow the Pilgrim Way, we rediscover the Spirit we thought had departed leading us forward, fresh, new and alive with the promise of resurrection. The great work of the times through which we are living is to find a new direction for all humanity, and that great work begins with a journey.

Richard Frazer
January 2025

FOREWORD

Few people can claim to have changed the course of history with respect to pilgrimage, but in a small way, as I shall share shortly, Richard Frazer is one of them. But first, early in this book, he remarks that no one 'does' the *Camino*. Rather, this ancient pilgrimage route through France and Spain to Santiago 'does' you.

With crisp narrative flow, we're led through nearly 700 miles – some 1,000 kilometres – of countryside and villages in daily walks and nightly stops at hostels, inns and monasteries. It's not just Richard's running up against his own physical limitations that's challenging. It's also the encounters with fellow travellers on the way. The ones who snore like weaving looms all night in dormitories. The ones who humble him with kindness, as if he'd met the patron saint along the route.

Richard loves observing human nature. In one scene, the conversation amongst strangers round the dinner table gets dominated by a pilgrim from Geneva. His commandeering questions draw the motley walkers into the practicalities of kit and boasts of daily mileage tallies. Everyone gets caught up by the competitive pull of his invasive mental field, until he throws his questions to a quiet and unassuming French lady. Why was she amongst them, round the table? Was it for spiritual reasons, or was she just an avid walker? She was there, she answered quietly, 'to give thanks'. Her answer served both as a soft rebuke and penetrating gift – not only to the brusque Genevan, but to them all.

Such are the anecdotes that interlace this book. There is a deeper stratum too. As he walks, Richard tries as best he can to avoid being found out that he's a clergyman. So much of the church, he says, has become an embarrassment. The institution trots trite dogmas out and gives unsatisfying answers to deep questions. Mostly it forgets its own complicity in violence, going back to Roman times and all those later holy wars. Here we encounter Richard as the Presbyterian minister. A Protestant in the spirit, as the name implies, the spirit of protest. A senior office-bearer in the Church of Scotland, standing in the shoes of militant Reformation theologians – yet one who sees the need within his own denomination to face up to and redress 'the cold, heartless impact' of a Calvinism that has too often been used to intimidate people.

It's not, he insists, that people aren't spiritual any more. It's more that bombast from Geneva – whether left over from the sixteenth century, or from an overbearing fellow pilgrim round the dinner table – no longer speaks to a younger generation that, with good reason, is sensitised to anything authoritarian. Today, it is in the recovery of spirituality, not religiosity, in which most seekers' yearning lies. There lies freedom of the soul, or as Richard puts it: 'To be a pilgrim you don't have to jump through hoops or sign up to doctrines you'd rather question – you just have to set off!'

He should know, indeed, the institution itself is waking up. Within the Church of Scotland as 'by law established', Richard convened the influential Church and Society Council, the committee charged with questions of faith and nationhood. This is where our intrepid walker's small but significant contribution to pilgrim history kicks in. He doesn't admit to it in this book, but in 2017, under his watch and with his theological input and encouragement, the church's General Assembly reversed its getting-on 500 years' hostility to pilgrimage. As its own theologians say, 'the Reformed church is always reforming itself', and here we saw that happening.

But what had been the original Protestant objection to pilgrimage? Not without some reason in their time, Reformation clergy such as Luther and Calvin held that pilgrimages commercialised religion. They kept the people off their work. Pilgrim shrines were funnels that channelled money away from local needs and back to Rome. Luther was the one who really laid it on. In 1520 in a grandiloquent address to the Christian nobility of Germany he had described pilgrimages as giving occasion for 'countless causes of sin'. Such peregrination around the countryside was to be done away with except, he conceded, when it was 'out of curiosity, to see cities and countries'. In other words, the peasants were to quit their holidays, but the nobility could keep their tourism. You could gallivant off to wherever you could afford, provided it was devoid of religious intent. That was for keeping firmly beneath the thumb of Luther's pulpit.

It has been this use of religion for psychological and political control that, as Richard diagnoses it, has closed the doors on faith for many. Far from being a trellis, a structure that leads the vine of spiritual life towards the light to ripen grapes and make good wine, organised religion has struggled to give life to many in our times. The vine has had to find its own wild way. That's where pilgrimage comes into play. As Richard told the *Daily Telegraph* when asked about the Kirk's formal rehabilitation of the practice: 'People who walk the Camino may not be conventionally religious, but very few who reach Santiago de Compostela would deny the journey there was a spiritual experience.'

The faithful if meandering stick with which he tapped his way to Santiago had been given to him in connection with his work amongst homeless people in Edinburgh's Grassmarket area. Reading this book, Richard himself at times becomes a homeless itinerant. A pilgrim journey, he tells us, 'can reconfigure our lives', drawing us into touch with places and their mix of human types along the way. The poet Walt Whitman, a vagabond *par excellence*, spoke of such encounters as 'letters from God dropped in the street, and every one is signed by God's name'.

'If the Camino has taught me anything,' Richard concludes, it is a 'commitment to working to build communities of trust and friendship which are free of prejudice and the abuse of power where people seek out the essential goodness and grace that is at the heart of all.'

There you see the message of this book. I wish you well, and every pleasure and reflection, in joining him along its way.

Alastair McIntosh
Author of *Soil and Soul* and *Poacher's Pilgrimage*

PROLOGUE
Meeting St Jacques

I hobbled into La Ferme du Barry, a pilgrim refuge in Aumont-Aubrac in the Cévennes region of France, a defeated man. Only three days into my pilgrimage from Le Puy-en-Velay to Santiago de Compostela, I was broken and utterly dejected. My knees were shot by the constant up and down of the hilly terrain, I had the worst dose of tendonitis I had ever known in my left ankle, and blisters covered the soles of both my feet. I felt totally crippled and doubted I could go on. I had arrived from Edinburgh only days before, and now felt I needed to get back on the train and head home with my tail between my legs, a humiliated man who'd completely misjudged his ability. I was rehearsing in my mind what I might say to all the people who'd supported me in this venture, how I'd tell them that it was all a big mistake and beyond me. I was also missing my family and ached for them in my misery.

What had I been thinking of? I really believed that in the seven weeks I'd given myself I could cover the 1,500 kilometres to Santiago. I wasn't just a fool, I was completely unrealistic. There had been such a build-up. Weeks of planning, though admittedly not a huge amount of long-distance training. Then there was the last-minute decision to buy a pair of lightweight boots rather than wearing the colossal but comfortable hiking boots that had served me well for the past few years. The day I left Le Puy I'd got soaked in a thunderstorm and set off with saturated feet. The lightweight boots had no waterproofing. I had been too self-assured – I thought I was fit and would be able to brag about the mileage I'd clock up each day, leaving all my poor fellow pilgrims in a cloud of dust behind me. I'd set off thinking I was in a race, and, like a greyhound out of a trap, I'd covered over 30 kilometres on my first day and had clocked up close to 100 kilometres by the time I got to La Ferme du Barry. Now I didn't know where to turn, except to disappear inside a bottle. And there were plenty of opportunities for that. The twenty-first-century pilgrim routes, like those of the Middle Ages, are well served for evening drinking.

The patron at La Ferme du Barry has a bit of a reputation on the Chemin de St Jacques, as the Camino is called in France. He was someone who seemed to me to be growling more than speaking. He had a permanent, slightly deranged grin on his face and a glint in his eye that led me to think that he saw me as a complete fool. Whatever language it was that he was speaking, it didn't sound French; Occitan, it might have been. He seemed timeless. I could imagine his great-great-grandfather-times-six offering the same gruff hospitality to pilgrims back in the Middle Ages.

I was in a terrible state. By some weird logic, I had thought that if I walked quickly I'd have more evening time to rest up and recover. I got changed, brooded over my feet and made, or should I say hobbled, my way into the village to explore and find a beer, the best anaesthetic known to man. I knew I needed to drown out the reality of my situation.

There is a beautiful church in Aumont-Aubrac dedicated to St Étienne. It has been wonderfully restored. Earlier in the day I had heard my first act of religious piety taking place on the Camino. As I was making my way along a picturesque country lane, I began to hear an unfamiliar sound. Was it a strange animal grazing in the field? As I got closer I realised that they were human voices and when closer still I heard singing, chanting in fact. As I passed the field where the sound was coming from, I saw three young monks and about three or four other young people huddled under a huge tree, obviously holding an act of worship. It was quite moving really, and they had chosen a lovely spot for their devotions. Now, sitting outside l'église St Étienne, the same little group I had passed earlier in the day arrived and walked wistfully into the church, presumably to round off their day with more prayer rather than beer, just the act of piety that I'd singularly failed to achieve throughout my life. A wave of inadequacy and guilt flooded over me to compound my wretched physical state, and I took a generous gulp of my anaesthetic.

The group stopped and chatted, and one of the monks very kindly informed me that they had received permission to say mass in the church the next morning and I would be very welcome to join them. Well, I wasn't going to turn down the first genuine and warm invitation to a Roman Catholic mass I had ever received. I was also taken with their genuine, palpable sense of holiness, an aura of gentle grace that, though I envied it in others, I realised I had also frequently sneered at in the past. I sat with my beer and reflected, in my wasted state of mind and body, on the ways that I have struggled with holiness over the years. I have frequently thought of piety as showy, prissy and a kind of affectation, but I have also failed to come to terms with the fact that such a perspective is far too judgemental. This group was utterly genuine. It all made me more self-reproachful and miserable.

After my beer, I headed back to La Ferme du Barry. The place was filling up with a selection of pilgrims. Not long after, the party of monks and their companions showed up; Franciscans, I thought.

Our host was famed across pilgrimage circles for his house speciality, *aligot*. It is a cheese and potato concoction that looks rather like paint in consistency. It is melted down and mixed in what looks like a giant paint tin. We sat down to eat, about 30 of us, in a wonderful, rustic setting. The wine flowed freely, as did the conversation in a large number of languages. I was able to communicate in Italian with a German woman who spoke no French and a French chap who had no English. It was wonderful to revive a bit of my rusty and underused Italian and even to begin to tune into a little of the French conversations around me.

That evening our table was one of great bonhomie, reviving my spirits a little. One of the guests was a German lady with a remarkable name, Halo. I had met her earlier in the day with her friend Hannah. They had grimaced sympathetically as they watched me slapping another blister plaster onto my raw feet. At dinner, they spoke about Meister Eckhart, who had said, back in the Middle Ages, that one's relationship to God had more to do with what was going on in our hearts than with our affiliation to a particular religious tradition. I'd read somewhere years before that our faith is much more the story of our longing than of our possessing. It seemed to me that the journey was a good metaphor for that longing to discover more and see what might be over the horizon, whilst the institutions we've created with all their doctrine and structure had more to do with possession.

I started to feel a bit better about my failure at piety, thinking that I was perhaps justified in not making any show of prayerfulness. My obvious preference for sitting in bars downing a beer rather than kneeling at prayer in picturesque rural churches could perhaps be justified by Eckhart's obvious preference for the inward, rather than the outward, expression of one's relationship with the Divine. We also spoke about the violence that can occur when people have too much disposable wealth and have not learned when enough is enough. In their view we can become brutal and even barbaric in our efforts to hold on to what we have, anxious about what might happen if we lose our material advantages. I grimaced when I thought about the advantage I was trying to give myself by racing through my Camino and how my excess consumption of alcohol that night was in stark contrast to those kindly, pious monks who stopped to pray and give thanks under trees and in lovely little country churches.

We spoke about my hopes for being a part of the revival of pilgrimage walking in Scotland, and all my fellow guests vowed to come to Scotland and explore it for themselves. We toasted the idea of pilgrimage as a spiritual exercise and generally had the most wonderful, convivial evening. I had arrived at La Ferme du Barry feeling a fraud, slightly out on a limb because I was hobbling around and everyone else looked fit and well. I was cursing my boots, or at least the fact that I had not done enough walking in them before I set off. Now, however, in spite of my self-reproachfulness, I felt once more a part of the pilgrimage community, included and accepted and with something to offer, and that, in itself, is a wonderful lesson of the democratic and inclusive nature of the pilgrim community. The hospitality of the table had rehabilitated my spirits at least, but my ankle and feet were still in a horrible mess. What could I do?

Nothing quite prepared me for what happened next.

As we turned in for the night, I was climbing into bed when a man named Jacques, who was walking with his niece, noticed my feet. 'My God,' he said. 'Look at your feet, you must be in a bad way.' Now Jacques was a tall and elegant man, a banker from Grenoble, and obviously a well-seasoned walker. He had a kind and honest face and was immediately the sort of person that you might trust as a guardian of your money. What he asked me to do, however, was to entrust my feet to him. 'I can help you,' he said. 'One of the things I love to do when walking is to look after other people's feet. It is my way of helping out. I would be honoured to take a look at your feet and see if I could be of assistance. I will not do anything that you do not want me to, but I have all the equipment with me. I always carry it for just this sort of eventuality.'

Well, I thought to myself, I am sure he cannot do any further harm. It seemed like a genuine offer of help. So I agreed. Meanwhile, Halo announced, 'I am a trained nurse, I will assist.'

The two of them set to work. In the gloom of the dormitory they donned head torches as though they were in theatre and the operation commenced. Hannah grimaced from her bunk in the background, offering soothing and encouraging words as Jacques, with great delicacy and gentleness, removed with a pair of scissors what looked like acres of damaged skin from my heels and soles. His approach to foot care was quite different to the blister-plaster approach. The plaster I had been using calls itself a second skin and it isolates the wound, sealing it off and giving you a kind of cushion. Jacques recommended lots of iodine to guard against infection. This, he announced, was vitally important. He also applied dressings made from breathable gauze with something called *tulle gras* and Parafix, which were made from petroleum-type products and were quite greasy. His point was that my feet needed to heal, free from infection and the suffocation of a plaster that did not permit the feet to breathe.

Earlier in the evening I'd had my first ever Skype conversation with my wife Kate on the mobile. She had immediately picked up on how low I was feeling about the state of my feet and had been insistent that I get them properly treated. By about midnight, I felt that that was exactly what had happened. We all turned in for the night and whilst my feet were still sore, I had the best night's sleep yet. I felt refreshed and uplifted by the kindness of strangers.

In the morning after breakfast, Jacques insisted that I had overdone things in the first days and that I needed to rest for a bit. My feet were still utterly raw and my tendon felt red hot. To keep walking in this state was a form of suicide. Jacques said I ought to take at least two days' rest. Neither the stress injury nor the blistered feet would heal if I kept going. He knew the very place to do this and advised that I should get a lift to a convent a little further along the Camino at a place called Saint-Côme-d'Olt. I made arrangements for the van that picks up people's bags and ferries pilgrims around to collect me later in the morning and 'take me to the convent'. Somehow, that had a nice ring to it. It felt really good to be a Scots Presbyterian minister, incognito, benefitting from respite in a convent. But before setting off, two more experiences occurred that morning that proved to be moving and rather wonderful. I'd heard it said that no one 'does' the Camino, it 'does' you. I was beginning to see what they meant. I was no longer fully in control of what was happening to me. The Camino experience was shaping me, as well as challenging me.

As I was packing up back in the dormitory after breakfast, I had a few minutes alone with Jacques. First of all, I told him, 'I came on the Chemin de St Jacques but I did not expect to meet St Jacques! Thank you for all your kindness and help last night. I think you have put me on the road to recovery.' He smiled broadly. It wasn't just the medical attention that I meant had helped, though it clearly had. It was a lesson in life that Jacques had taught me. His intervention felt almost like a small miracle. In my conceit, I had set off on this walk as if it were a competition. I had smugly passed fellow pilgrims at a cracking pace and had been taking a perverse satisfaction in discovering that I was doing in two days what some pilgrims had been doing in three or four. But a pilgrimage is not a race. I realised that I was being very silly and that I had absolutely no idea of the spirit of the pilgrim. I was in sports mode, knocking off the miles with hardly a moment to breathe in the atmosphere of the places I was walking through or take the time just to be, to absorb and to connect with myself, other people and the environment.

The tenderness with which Jacques had treated my feet had been quite a moving experience. I had felt quite vulnerable as he had worked on them. There was a real sense of having been ministered to, something similar to the experience that Jesus's disciples must have had when, on the night before his arrest, he'd removed his outer robe, stooped down and washed their feet. Until this moment, I had always thought that it was Jesus who'd made himself vulnerable by assuming the role of a servant. But there was a vulnerability that came to me as Jacques tended to me. For the first time, I began to see that allowing others to take care of you is a moment of taking the risk of trust in the kindness of another. I realised how rarely I had done that kind of thing, having always been largely self-sufficient and almost never feeling that I needed help.

Jacques said, 'You have to look after yourself if you want to look after others.' He didn't know what I did for a living, but it was a remarkable observation. Jacques and Halo had shown immense kindness. They were like the Good Samaritan, who had taken the time to attend to the man who'd been robbed and left for dead in a ditch. I had been so set on getting to my destination that probably, if I had seen a man lying in the ditch, I would have walked past on the other side, just like the priest and the Levite in the story. I felt so ugly, so unworthy to be making this journey. Here I was hobbling around planning to take some time out holed up in a convent whilst it seemed everyone else was in crashing form. Far from being the helper, the one in charge and competent and ready to be a shoulder to cry on as I usually was back at home, I was discovering what it felt like to be in need.

And then an extraordinary thing happened.

Jacques had found my comment likening him to St Jacques quite amusing. But I realised that he was also quite moved too. 'You seem,' he began, 'to be someone whom I could perhaps talk to, someone that I could ask a favour of, trusting that you might not laugh or be embarrassed. You see, I have come on this walk for a reason.' He then shared with me some of the difficulties he was facing in his own personal life. He was using the journey to come to terms with all that had happened to him in recent months. He continued, 'I have no one who really understands, who knows what this loneliness feels like. I sometimes feel I just need another man to hug me. I know this might sound odd, but you seem to be someone I could ask this of. Do you think that now, we could just embrace, man to man, for a moment, before we set off? Some reassurance that I am not a terrible man would be a great help to me.'

And there, in that dormitory, Jacques and I had a moment when we embraced. It was a simple, I would say beautiful, encounter. Nothing about it felt odd, or inappropriate. It lasted for all of ten seconds and then I saw a little bit of the weight that Jacques was carrying had been lifted from him, his face had brightened and he was steeled a little if only for the challenges of the coming day. I hoped that this encounter had perhaps been a little source of healing for him too. It felt good in some way to repay his kindness of the previous night.

I suppose this is quite a difficult thing for many men to do, on reflection. It has not always been a 'man's thing', and yet how much acceptance and human warmth can be conveyed when an embrace is given and received in the right context? It also makes you wonder just how much weight people carry through life, never quite able to ask a friend to share the load. One of the things that I like to see is the young men and women of my children's generation being far more physical with each other than my generation ever has been. I feel sure this is a good thing.

In these last few hours, the Camino had taught me some really important lessons in life. First of all, the importance of pacing ourselves. If we want to have a lively hope of reaching our destination then we should avoid setting off at a pace that will lead to burnout after only a short while. How often do we go through life never thinking what it might take to sustain ourselves for the long haul? The second lesson was one about our tendency to be self-reliant. I often charge at life and don't accept help or think I need it. Here I found two strangers willing to take the time to help me and, as a result of my willingness to accept that help, I had, in turn, had the privilege of being able to help Jacques in some small way, because, even in such a short time, a relationship of trust had built up between us. Jacques then left La Ferme du Barry and I never saw him again. It felt as though I had met an angel with a healing touch and an important message to share. Was this real?

All this had happened in the space of a few hours, and when I left for the mass at l'église St Étienne a few moments later I remembered that Jacques had asked me to pray for him. I knew that though I would probably never see him again, that was fine and the right thing to do. He had a lot of stuff to resolve. I had indeed met St Jacques, and for all the setback of my injuries, and perhaps because of them, this journey was already becoming a true pilgrimage.

At the church, my hunch, indeed my naïve certainty, that these monks were Franciscans was quickly quashed. I clearly do not know my monks. It turns out they were Carmelites. Monk-spotting could be as much fun as bird-watching in certain places with the right guidebook. In fact, somewhere amongst the ridiculous accumulation of books that I have hoarded over the years I have a guidebook to ecclesiastical dress. What on earth for, I wonder?

The mass was beautiful and very moving. There was a lot of toing and froing with much fiddling and fussing and long pauses between different elements of the service. These monks were quite young, and it occurred to me, as a seasoned celebrant of the sacraments, that maybe their fiddling about wasn't so much ritual as inexperience, made more complex by an unfamiliar setting.

One of them clearly forgot to put wine in the cup, started saying the holy words over it, realised his mistake and then went back to his chum to fill it up. Maybe this was all part of the liturgy; who knows? None of this did anything to spoil what was a moving occasion shared by about 20 pilgrims. It was all done in French, but the wonder of the mass is that even I could follow so many of the words and (some) of the actions we in the Church of Scotland share in common.

I have always been quite fascinated by liturgy, which really just means the stuff that happens in worship, otherwise known as ritual. Some habits and ways of doing things in church have a very practical rather than spiritual justification. Was incense a way of neutralising the odoriferous nature of unwashed worshippers, gathered into a single space, I wonder? As another example, in some traditions, the words of the prayers might be sung by the priest. One of the things I have learned over the years is that big, barn-like churches often have terrible acoustics for the spoken voice. If you sing a prayer, you are much more likely to be heard. I think that's where the sing-song Anglican voice you sometimes hear comes from: it stems from the fact that electric sound systems have only been around for a relatively short time and people had to find other ways to be heard.

The central part of the liturgy that most people know is the communion, the sharing of bread and wine that Jesus did on the night he was betrayed and arrested. Christians have been doing that since before they had Bibles, which is an interesting point to make to fellow Reformed Presbyterians who have often made a much bigger thing of the Bible than of the communion. In John's Gospel, on that last night before his arrest, Jesus doesn't share bread and wine; instead he washes his disciples' feet. A priest friend of mine pointed out recently that the Christian church might have been quite a different organisation if we washed each other's feet every week! Of course, the other great liturgical practice, handed down since this happened to Jesus in the River Jordan, is baptism, the use of cleansing water as a sign of being included in the Christian community. Not many do it in rivers any more, just a wee splash of water from a silver bowl, but I loved the moment years ago when Ian Macfarland, Lutheran pastor and theologian, leant over to me as I was about to baptise his daughter and whispered, 'Use plenty of water!'

Another friend told me that in the Free Church tradition of the West Highlands of Scotland people often think that 'liturgy' has been replaced by, often interminable, preaching. But my friend pointed out that there is a whole liturgical practice that goes on around the Sabbath, from scrubbing boots and putting on your best clothes to walking the long miles to the kirk instead of using the car and tying up the swings in the play park to ensure they are not used out of respect for the Sabbath. Liturgy is just the actions that people do that enable worship and reverence, so why not add to it by walking great distances?

In spite of the slightly haphazard nature of the liturgy that morning, I was also beginning to understand what someone had meant when they said that the real liturgy happens outside the church. Because whatever was going on in this slightly clumsy church service in Aubrac that morning, the real liturgy had happened in that dormitory at La Ferme du Barry over these last hours. So, my prayer for Jacques didn't really amount to anything very liturgical. I simply held him in my thoughts for a while, with a feeling of gratitude for our encounter and his kindness, and maybe even a sense of appreciation that the setbacks that I'd had were gifts too. Then I lit some candles, for Jacques and the challenge he was facing in his personal life, my family and my poor dad, now terribly frail as he entered his ninetieth year.

On our way out of the church, I chatted with an American pilgrim and told him I had seen these chaps in a field the previous day at their prayers. 'Yes,' came the reply. 'These Carmelites are immersed in the Bible and prayer.' That is great, I thought, again reflecting on my own lack of meaningful piety. I am sure that they are immersed in this journey too. It felt to me on this morning, only three days in, that the Camino was getting a hold of me, that far from it being an experience that I was having on my own terms, the Camino was working on me and doing its own thing to me, reading me, testing me, probing my vulnerability and teaching me. Of course, I think that this is one of the great lessons that the pilgrim will learn if he or she is open: that the journey starts to read us rather than the other way about. The Camino has a life and agenda all of its own, and if you enter into it with an open heart – and even if you don't – it will have its own way with you. What you get out of it might not be what you expect at all.

CHAPTER 1
Setting Off

Scottish writer and poet Nan Shepherd wrote a wonderful book about her deep knowledge and experience of the Cairngorm massif. She spent many years ranging over those hills and, far from 'bagging the tops', she got to know the entire landscape and the mystical connections that the mountains made with her interior self. She often described herself as a pilgrim rather than a hillwalker and, instead of observing and writing about the landscape, much of her writing is about the inner journey, the realisation that 'going out was really a going in', as John Muir, the great Scottish conservationist and inspirer of the American National Parks, famously put it. I first encountered John Muir in Arizona when I was hiking down into the Grand Canyon. Sitting in a climbers' bar after a remarkable couple of days exploring this vast chasm, I came across one of his quotes on the wall. Apparently, on seeing the Grand Canyon for the first time, he had exclaimed, 'An ostentatious gesture, even for God.' How gloriously Presbyterian!

Nan Shepherd shared something of that Scottish reserve when she reflected on her own approach to the hills. In *The Living Mountain* she wrote, 'The pilgrim contents herself always with looking along and inwards to mystery, where the mountaineer longs to look down and outwards onto total knowledge.' I had spent years, ever since I was in the

Cub Scouts in fact, bagging Munros, ticking off the Scottish hills above 3,000 feet. My first pilgrimage walk, the Machar March, we had called it, was in the 1990s, walking from the island of Iona to the ancient Celtic cathedral of St Machar in Old Aberdeen, where I was minister at the time. I had begun on that walk to understand the difference between a purposeful journey through a landscape as opposed to the genuine joy of, rather at random, selecting the next Munro on my life list, getting to the top, 'looking down' and then heading back to where I had started. The humble, mystical journey of the pilgrim from one place to another was beginning to make more sense to me than the idea of bagging all the Scottish Munros.

I was starting my epic journey to Santiago, but not in a wild landscape journeying inward to peace and inner enlightenment; rather in Paris, heading for my chosen start point at Le Puy-en-Velay, quite baffled and anxious as to how to negotiate the Métro to start the next stage of my train journey that had begun that morning in Edinburgh. I had to get from Gare du Nord to Gare du Lyon to head south.

I found myself quite short of time and searching rather aimlessly around the station looking for the right platform. I often find that complex charts and lists of information are quite intimidating and can even make me panic a little. I took a chance and headed off purposefully in a certain direction, the one that 'felt' most right. As I sat on the train, the fog of my panic began to clear and I scanned around to see if I could find out if I was heading for Gare du Lyon after all. Perhaps I was well on my way to Charles de Gaulle airport. I really had no idea. After a few minutes, I made some sense of the map on the train and I realised that I was, by some miracle, only two stops away from Gare du Lyon – a triumph of instinct over reason!

I was duly deposited in the correct station and made my way towards another baffling electronic noticeboard. I felt very self-conscious with my Camino stick in hand, but for the first time I encountered people who guessed what I was about. The man at the ticket counter asked me if I was off to do the Chemin de St Jacques. A triumphant, cheerful exchange in broken, terrible French ensued, but it felt good to be on my way. I hopped onto the TGV bound for Lyon, catching a glimpse of some of the wonderful familiar sights of Paris and also some particularly depressing high-rise housing before the train gathered pace and turned everything into a blur.

We were in Lyon within two hours of leaving Paris and, with uncharacteristic ease, I boarded a train for Saint-Étienne and then caught the last train of the day from Saint-Étienne for Le Puy. There were only about four passengers on board, and we headed off at a more sedate pace than the TGV, but none the less in a swish and rather elegant carriage. As I settled into my seat, I became conscious of a man (actually the only other person in my part of the train) looking in my direction, or more specifically looking at my Camino stick. This object was clearly going to be something of a celebrity, so I had better explain its provenance.

A few years before we had begun to develop the Grassmarket Community Project for vulnerable adults in Edinburgh, I had decided that it might be fun to organise a pilgrimage walk to raise funds for the project. My two pilgrim friends from Aberdeen, Bill and Peter, with whom I had done the Machar March, readily agreed to come along, but this time we decided to open the walk to a wider group and included in our party some of the members of the project, some of whom had experience of homelessness. The route we chose took us from the door of Greyfriars Kirk, where I am minister, in central Edinburgh to the island of Lindisfarne, or Holy Island, in Northumberland. It was a great walk, full of adventures. Some people dropped out because they had physical difficulties or found the whole thing mentally trying. But, for each one of us, the experience was transformative and enriching and culminated in a wonderful gathering on the island when a busload of friends from the kirk and the project joined us for a picnic on the last day.

On the first day, as we departed from Greyfriars, we were met by Mary, a colleague and friend of my wife Kate, who had done a chunk of the Camino de Santiago as a part of her celebration of her fiftieth birthday and had been taking pupils from her school there for many years. She had acquired the stick in question on the Camino, and it had been for her something of a talisman. She was keen that I should carry the stick on this pilgrimage walk. I still remember her catching up with us on the canal towpath in Edinburgh in drenching rain and handing it over.

One of our party, John, had many years of drug addiction behind him and was a heavy smoker. I will never forget the look on his face as we ascended into the Pentland Hills above Edinburgh at Bonaly. I think he seriously thought he was going to die. He wavered and almost gave up at that point. A couple of days later, after a particularly long walk from Peebles to Melrose, he slumped down on a bunk in Melrose Youth Hostel and lit up a cigarette. The look on his face was certainly one of exhaustion, but it was also one of defiance. He may have been utterly drained but his look said, 'If you think I am going to walk outside to smoke this fag, you can forget it and I will probably murder you if you suggest it.' He had another wobble the next day but recovered himself, and it was a true inspiration to see his determination and fight to make it to Holy Island.

It was decided that the Camino stick would be awarded at the beginning of each of the ensuing days to the person who had performed best on the previous day, and it was John who carried the stick triumphantly for the next three days, all the way to the Northumberland coast, across the mud of low tide and onto the famous island. If ever I had wondered about the transformative power of walking, then this experience had confirmed to me that pilgrimage has the capacity to turn people's lives around. Whether or not the walk played its part, it's wonderful to know that John is now sorted out, walking regularly in the hills and maintaining a calm and ordered life following years of chaos and unhappiness in the wilderness of addiction.

So the stick seemed to attract a bit of a following. It was as though it carried with it the adventures it had been party to and transmitted its little signals to the people who came into contact with it. I had no donkey to act as a conversation piece as Robert Louis Stevenson had when he arrived in the Cévennes in the 1870s with Modestine, his obstinate and singular four-legged walking companion. This stick was a good substitute.

'You are a pilgrim?' my new friend on the train asked, or, rather, announced. Clearly it is only pilgrims who carry such rustic wooden sticks and I wondered if perhaps the possession of modern, ergonomic poles precluded one from true pilgrim status. Later on I came to understand that a true pilgrim doesn't give himself that designation; it is in the gift of others to call him a pilgrim. An interesting thought, and I thoroughly approve.

'You will need your stick for fending off the dogs,' my friend continued. 'How far are you going?'

'Well,' I replied, in terrible French, 'I hope to make it all the way to Santiago, but I have only seven weeks.' My friend winced at this, and came over to join me. He was a man in his fifties, healthy-looking, as though he kept himself fit by regular exercise. He had longish hair still in its original colour and gave me the impression that he might be just a few years older than me. My imagination took flight, thinking that he was probably a radical student in the late 1960s.

To my relief when he came to join me, it turned out that Grégoire was from Marseille and his English was rather good. We began a conversation about our respective plans. Grégoire was walking too, but had only a few days. As we chatted I interrogated him about pilgrim etiquette on the Chemin de St Jacques. I had to admit I had read a good deal about the Spanish section of the walk but very little about the French part. He informed me, for example, and I groaned inwardly at this, that I really ought to phone ahead each night to book accommodation. He told me that the way suddenly gets very busy at the border in Saint-Jean-Pied-de-Port and that if I was keen to do the conventional pilgrimage route I should be prepared to be in considerable company for most of the way, as the whole thing had become immensely popular, if not congested, over the last few years. He was far too polite to say it, but his wince I took to be an indication that if I thought I would make it all the way from Le Puy to Santiago in seven weeks, I was barking mad. He was right.

We soon arrived in Le Puy-en-Velay. It was after 10 p.m. by now and the town had gone to sleep. I realised that I had eaten almost nothing the whole day except what Kate had given me as a packed lunch that morning in Edinburgh. I announced, rather tactlessly, that I was starving and wondered out loud if there was anywhere to get something to eat. It turned out that Grégoire was heading to the same gîte; he had a little pasta and some tomatoes and onions in his sack, and kindly said that he would be happy to cook us both a meal.

And so, I met my first angel of the Camino. We had a simple but altogether delicious meal al fresco at our gîte. I managed to procure a couple of beers from the receptionist just before she clocked off for the night, and we sat under the stars eating a very fine plate of pasta and sipping beer. It felt like a magical and auspicious first night.

As the evening wore on and midnight approached I made a fateful mistake and asked Grégoire what he did for a living. 'I have forgotten what I do,' was his only reply, giving me the very strong impression that, whilst walking, he preferred to leave his other life behind. I had breached one more rule of the Camino: 'Don't pry into people's private lives.' It did of course get me speculating that my new friend was a Marseillais gangster or hit man on the run. But I actually have a sneaking suspicion he might have been a pastor. I don't know why I thought that, and I will never know, but some of the things he said suggested to me a man of considerable spirituality. And he wouldn't be the first minister to be mistaken for a gangster! We parted friends (he was none the wiser about my occupation either) and I felt hugely grateful for the nourishment of both good food and good conversation, retiring to bed blissfully unaware of the adventures that lay in wait for me and my Camino stick the following day.

CHAPTER 2
Le Puy-en-Velay

The morning dawned bright and sunny, but the air was thick and smelled of rain. I had a modest breakfast of the sort you expect in a French gîte with a café attached: coffee, orange juice and a croissant. As I ventured outside, I could see blue sky in one direction and ominous thick black clouds in another. The weather was definitely not promising. I made my way back to my room to pick up my kit, and by the time I had gathered all my bits and pieces together great droplets of rain were bouncing off the windows and rattling onto the cobbles below. It was the beginning of a monstrous deluge. All hell let loose with thunder, lightning and hail.

I pulled out my ridiculous rain cape from my pack and proceeded to try to cover myself in it. Now, this needs a bit of explaining. I had decided that in order to save weight I would not bring a rain jacket. I had a naïve hope that I wouldn't need it because it would be far too warm and it wouldn't rain. This was the Continent after all, and it was still summer: it was not supposed to rain or get cold. For about £2 I had bought a blue luminous poncho, actually just a giant, thin plastic bag with a small hood for my head. I had also brought my leather 'cowboy hat', goodness only knows why. By the time I made it to the cathedral, which, in such a precipitous town as Le Puy, is remarkably hard to find, even though it sits on top of a hill, my hat was completely saturated and stayed wet for the best part of the next four days. I grew to resent and then to hate that hat, as not only was it now a ton weight; it was also unbelievably uncomfortable. It was eventually dispatched home in a box along with a number of other articles that proved surplus to requirements in the early stages of my walk; and by the time I had lost and mislaid many other items in the early days, I realised that I'd had absolutely no concept of travelling light.

I began to understand why Stevenson had resorted to the delights of Modestine, the pack mule, as the perfect antidote to the indecisive pilgrim who cannot make tough choices about what to leave behind. Incidentally, on the way to the cathedral through this utter deluge, I managed to spot a postcard in a little shop window that showed the route that he had taken that had produced that wonderful classic *Travels with a Donkey*. It was now actually a *grande randonnée*: in France people were following in the footsteps of the famous Scot and sending postcards home to their loved ones showing his route, whilst in his homeland the book was almost completely forgotten.

I squelched into the cathedral in a state of complete saturation. The poncho might have kept me 'dryish', but because of the wide-brimmed nature of my leather hat, the run-off had poured down various gaps and crevices in the voluminous plastic poncho that did not quite fit over my rucksack. I realised that I was probably wetter than I might have been had I worn no protection whatsoever. I dripped and dribbled my way through the cathedral, leaving little pools of water at every point where I stopped. In the subdued light of the building, which at this time of the morning was almost completely empty, I felt as though I was as unwelcome as a slug in a vegetable patch.

After much meandering and some random backtracking, I found the place I was looking for, the cathedral shop, where, according to the information I had gleaned from my guidebook, I would be able to purchase my *créanciale* or pilgrim passport, the document that gets stamped each night and proves that you are a genuine pilgrim with all the rights and privileges that bestows. My meandering had been caused by the fact that the shop was hard to find because it was closed and was not due to open until 10 a.m. That was almost an hour hence. I took comfort from sitting under a statue of St Jacques himself in the cathedral. In this wooden carving he was wearing a very suitable poncho, not dissimilar in shape to my own but one that looked far more serviceable. He also, like me, carried a staff, but I'm sure his hat was not made of the same kind of porous leather as mine. I felt quite jealous, but also marginally reassured as, in spite of my assessment of his equipment as being somewhat better thought-through than mine and of a better standard (amazing for a first-century Palestinian wayfarer to get his kit so right for the fickle European climate), I realised that we looked surprisingly alike.

I composed a prayer and left it in the book for this purpose and lit four candles, one for Kate and one each for our children, and then settled down to have a good read of my guidebook, something I should have done long ago, but other things had got in the way as they always do. As I pulled the now soggy guidebook out in the dim light of the cathedral on this grey morning, I realised that I could not read a thing. My glasses! I rummaged around my pack and there was no sign of them. I had to retrace my steps back to the gîte in the torrential rain. In my misery, I let rip at the sky with an unselfconscious abandon. It felt as though someone was playing tricks, trying to thwart my hare-brained escapade and make me fail at the first hurdle. My feet were soaked through and I realised that the shoes I had bought, highly recommended as they were, were going to be utterly useless in any kind of damp conditions.

I rounded the corner to our gîte and a small Renault car with three young men inside came roaring past and straight through the most gigantic puddle. The wall of water that overwhelmed me would not have been out of place coming from a water cannon. It almost knocked me off my feet and I had to concede that it would have been churlish of me to deny these young men their snigger at the aftermath. It was total comedy.

Back in my room I took the opportunity to wring out my clothes and then searched every corner in vain for my glasses. And then, there they were – in the bottom of the rucksack that I had with me at the cathedral. Downstairs, I met Grégoire, who was having a leisurely breakfast and looked like he was going nowhere that day.

I was focused on Santiago and needed to get cracking even if it was still bucketing down. So I headed back to the cathedral, and by now I was becoming familiar with the damp streets of Le Puy. I spotted a couple of inviting-looking artisan shops, a boulangerie and a charcuterie, and I purchased some bread, a French sausage and a bit of cheese for my lunch and then headed into the cathedral once more, leaving my telltale trails behind me. By now it was 9.50 a.m. and the shop was open. I purchased my *créanciale* and beamed vacuously at the girl behind the counter as though I was the first person ever to attempt this mad adventure of walking to Santiago from Le Puy. Of course, it was the Bishop of Le Puy, Godescalc, who first did the walk in AD 951 and got the whole business of the Camino off the ground. Millions have done it since.

I stood in the cathedral rearranging my kit and squirreling away my *créanciale* to ensure that this now valuable document, the record of my walk, did not get a soaking and smudge all the lovely stamps with which I anticipated filling up the blank boxes. The nice girl had given me my first stamp, so I was on my way, or so I thought. But the Camino stick had other ideas. As I was making a few final adjustments before heading out once more into the rain, I let go of the stick momentarily. Below me was a metal grating and the stick managed to find its way down. I watched in horror as it began to disappear into the bowels of the cathedral. I had the impression, all in a moment, that some future archaeologist would dig it up one day and try to pass it off as a genuine medieval artefact. And just as that thought passed through my mind, I bent down and snatched it back up into the twenty-first century an instant before it vanished from view.

I made my way down some stunning steps and out into the rain and precipitous terrain of Le Puy, this ancient city built amongst volcanic outcrops. Indeed one of them has a chapel, dedicated to St Michel d'Aiguilhe (St Michael of the Needles) built precariously on its top by Godescalc to commemorate his pilgrimage all those years ago. I have to confess that in the rain and confusion of my first day, I wasn't in the mood to be a tourist and mooch around the town, I wanted to be off. As is my wont, I set off in completely the wrong direction. I was still trying to get my head around the breathtakingly simple device that the French use for telling pilgrims they are on the right track. It is a simple pair of red-and-white horizontal stripes. If you are about to turn there is a third white stripe with a little point, either to left or right, and, if you have gone the wrong way the two stripes are crossed – easy! Somehow, something so obvious and logical takes an age to register in my brain and I found myself meandering around the town desperately lost and frustrated.

At one point I spotted some fellow pilgrims and tried to give the impression that I was merely window shopping, rather than following them in order to find my way out of this wretched town. 'Aye right,' I muttered to myself, 'I am out here getting soaked with the intention of loading up my rucksack with useless tourist tat that I will then proceed to carry all the way to Santiago. If they believe that then I am the Pope.' When the pilgrims had passed I started to follow them for a few hundred yards until I realised that they were lost too. 'My God, this is not going well,' I said again, out loud, to no one in particular. I was now not just saturated, I was also beginning to feel cold. I thought I might end up with flu. I needed to crack on and get into my stride or else I would probably end up weeping uncontrollably on the ground and heading straight back to Scotland.

Eventually, I found the way, which turned out to be back past the gîte. How did I miss that, I wondered? I missed it because, a) I had failed to read my guidebook, which would have told me that the gîte was on the pilgrim way and b) I was still incapable of reading these wretchedly simple signs. Perhaps it was the high emotion and drama of everything, not to mention that extraordinary sense of anticipation that I'd had at the outset of a great adventure like this. I knew that I needed to clock off a few miles just to calm down a bit. The first few miles of the route took me steadily uphill. Notwithstanding the charms of Le Puy that

I had mostly missed, I followed the biblical imperative and, unlike the wife of Lot, never looked back. Thankfully, as I left Le Puy the rain began first to ease and then to stop. My hat still weighed a ton and had begun to irritate me so intensely that I wanted to fling it into the hedgerow. I was convinced I was walking through some charming countryside but the mist clung to every hill and filled every gully, so I had no real sense of the shape of the landscape or of what was going on in it.

As morning turned to afternoon, the sun came out, the mist cleared and I began to see the French countryside for the first time. I stopped to eat my lunch and change my socks, trying to dry the wet ones by hanging them from the Camino stick, but they were not going to dry in a hurry. My lunch gave me a delightful sense of continuity with pilgrims and peasants of the past as I imagined that the food I was eating – the cheese, bread and sausage – was not much different from that which people had been eating in this region for centuries.

As well as the food, another aspect of the Chemin de St Jacques that soon became apparent was the stone and metal crosses that marked the route of the pilgrimage at regular intervals. These markers, especially the stone ones, were absolutely ancient. They remind you that you're walking in the footsteps of past pilgrims and that the route has remained largely unchanged for a thousand years. Today, people worry about the 'relevance' of the church and there are all sorts of new initiatives springing up in order to connect with a new generation, but sometimes the best new ideas are old ones that are rediscovered, such as the idea of following in the footsteps of pilgrims who have made the same journey over a millennium.

The last seven kilometres to Monistrol-d'Allier were the hardest of the day. After a wee place called Saint-Privat-d'Allier there is a massive climb over the hill until you drop back down to the river once more. I stopped in Saint-Privat for a deliciously cool drink and met a friendly English family on holiday who had absolutely no idea they were in pilgrim country. (Actually, I don't think they knew what a pilgrim was!)

By now, it was really quite hot. I set off up the hill. After a few hundred yards of slog, I suddenly realised to my horror that my hand was empty of the Camino stick. I made a quick about-turn and found it propped against the wall of the café.

At the top of the hill were the remains of a very imposing thirteenth-century castle, Rochegude, and I speculated that this might be my first encounter with the Knights Templar, that ancient chivalric order which guaranteed the safety of medieval pilgrims, but who were disbanded by the Pope around the thirteenth century for getting too powerful and apparently for worshipping cats, indulging in homosexual acts and a host of other 'crimes' against the law of the church. Their demise has, of course, provoked the emergence of all sorts of fantasies, plots and conspiracy theories.

The woods through which I now descended were still wet and slippery after the day's rain, and for the first time the stick actually came in handy. Monistrol-d'Allier, my first stop on the way from Le Puy, seemed impossibly low down in the valley below. Eventually, it must have been around 5 p.m., I arrived in the village.

Once again, I had one of my mental blocks and marched up to a gîte called Tsabonne and announced myself as one of their guests for the night. 'I'm afraid not. We are fully booked,' announced the lady at the desk. 'Indeed, I told your wife that when I spoke to her on the telephone.' It then dawned on me: Kate had phoned ahead to book my first two nights' accommodation, and I now remembered that she had tried two places here. I was in fact booked into a place back round the corner. Off I headed, rather sheepishly, to a slightly grubby place on the main road. 'It was, you may say, satisfactory,' in the ironic words of T.S. Eliot's Magi when they found the stable in which Jesus was born. The people at the gîte clearly had no idea that I was expected and yet had plenty of room. So I had my first night in a bunk room on the Camino, sharing it with a young French couple whom I feel sure would much rather have had the room to themselves.

Over supper, the young couple appeared, as did another much older and very chatty lady. I stumbled and spattered my way through a conversation with them and even managed to elicit the kind offer of the use of a mobile phone to send Kate a text, since in this valley my phone was completely without signal. That night I slept fitfully as someone on the floor above appeared to be pacing around throughout the entire night. I always imagine in such circumstances that the owners of places like this must be up to no good if they are so active in the small hours. 'Are they chopping up the bodies of pilgrims?' I speculated, but failed to convince myself that this might be the case. I wasn't going to get spooked. At least not until tomorrow.

CHAPTER 3
The Beast of Gévaudan

At breakfast, I realised to my horror that the stick was missing again. I flapped around thinking I had left it outside the gîte overnight. I cast an accusing eye over my fellow inmates, imagining that they might have conspired to relieve me of it in the night. Eventually, the entire population of the gîte was engaged in a systematic search of parts of the building I could not possibly have visited, but to no avail: the stick was gone. I felt a pang of guilt and a real sense of having failed in my responsibility towards Mary and her gift. I had hardly begun and already I had lost the stick. In a mood of despondency I set off, only to be waylaid by a small group of Tsabonne residents. One of them asked: 'Did you leave your stick outside Tsabonne last night? I thought it might be yours because I remember seeing you when you arrived and it had a little bit of tartan attached to it. It's still there, propped up on the wall outside the gîte.' My heart soared; I was beginning to be emotionally attached to it. I turned the corner and there it was, leaning nonchalantly against the wall, ready for the day.

It was a steep climb up to the region known as Le Domaine du Sauvage. I passed a good number of people on the way. Many must have been from Tsabonne, and they remarked on the stick as I passed. It had obviously made quite an impact. I felt quite proud. It was only later in the day that I discovered that I had left my ultra-light tartan trousers, my 'evening wear' back at the gîte. It was becoming clear that I needed to get a grip!

And now for Le Domaine du Sauvage and the Beast of Gévaudan...

It is a heck of a pull out of the gorge that the River Allier makes at Monistrol. Ever a glutton for punishment, I always see a steady climb as a challenge to be met head on and the sweatier the better. It is, I am afraid to say, probably a bit of an ego thing, that I paced uphill, refused to rest and passed weary pilgrims along the way with a smug inner gleefulness. Halfway up out of the gorge I received a message from Kate (mobile signal restored) which included a photo of my dad, very frail but smiling in his checked shirt.

One of the few stories about my father's experience in the Second World War that any of my family have managed to get out of him is that he walked all the way from Salerno to Austria in the south-west of Italy, in the course of the last two years of the war. He landed with the invading Allied forces and, while they waited offshore for the signal to land, my father, who was a strong swimmer, was asked to give some of the soldiers swimming lessons. The reason was that when the landing craft arrived on the beaches, not all of them would make it to dry land and it was helpful if the soldiers could swim at least a few feet to the shore. The journey on foot to Austria took a considerable length of time, with a protracted stopover at the siege of Monte Cassino, one of the bloodiest battles of the war. Now that he was elderly, frail and weak, there was a degree to which I felt I was doing this walk for him. Kate reported that messages about my progress seemed to be the only thing he was interested in.

I remember reading many years ago about the German film director Werner Herzog. He was a great friend of the film critic Lotte Eisner. Herzog lived in Munich and received a message from Paris that Eisner was gravely ill. His message back was, 'Hold on, I am coming.' He then set off and walked all the way to Paris from his home in Munich. When he arrived she was fully recovered. I wonder whether the wonderful novel *The Unlikely Pilgrimage of Harold Fry* by Rachel Joyce might have been inspired by this story. Both are beautiful, quirky tales that hint at the mysterious healing power of walking. Somehow, in spite of the fact that my dad wasn't communicating much by now, I got the impression that he was rooting for me on my walk, and I was rooting for him as he languished bedridden back in Edinburgh.

As I made my way out of the gorge there were a number of small farms and a little hamlet, Montaure. The hamlet stood on the edge of a rather bleak moor, somewhat reminiscent of Scotland. As though anticipating the thirst that climbing up from the Allier might induce, there was a small tap very prominently in evidence with a sign, '*eau potable*', attached to one of the farm buildings. It was a welcome opportunity to fill up and get some much-needed refreshment. An old farmer with a kindly face was wandering about like retired farmers the world over often do, dressed for work and looking busy just tinkering. This old chap must have been as old as my dad. He beamed at me and muttered a few words that I could not comprehend, but he concluded with '*Bon courage!*' That I did understand.

However, it had the effect of slightly unsettling me. Why would I need courage, I thought to myself? I realised that, lurking in the back of my mind as I faced the prospect of this blasted moor, was the story of the Beast of Gévaudan, not to mention the long road to Santiago. The entire population of this region had been terrorised for several years in the eighteenth century by a mad wolf-like creature who had torn the throats out of its victims. Usually, the Beast set on people going about their business alone. I guess that a solitary pilgrim must have been fair game. There was a particularly nasty episode in which at least 200 people had been attacked, many killed, some partially eaten by the Beast. It was claimed that it was a werewolf, but others thought it might have been the product of a mating between a large mastiff dog and a wolf. Professional hunters were dispatched from Paris. Eventually the Beast was slain and the attacks stopped.

The whole affair gripped the nation, and even a century later Robert Louis Stevenson in his travels through the Cévennes was made aware of the reputation of this area and reassured himself with 'one of the best cigarettes of my experience' in the middle of the night as sleep eluded him on a wild and windy night under the stars. Whatever, I felt something of a chill as I waved to this old farmer and headed off. I had no urge to smoke a cigarette as Stevenson had done when spooked by stories of the Beast, however. Having been a smoker in my youth and having really enjoyed it, the whole process from rolling the perfect fag to the gut churning nausea of the first drag of the day, I now knew I had won back my lungs and nothing was going to let me lose them to the dreaded weed once more.

As I walked on, I noticed something that is quite important for walkers to bear in mind. On one level you are travelling at three miles per hour and the landscape is slow to change, but at other times, it can be surprising how quickly the scenery can shift as you are walking through it. If I disappeared off into a 'dwam', when I woke up it would often feel that I was in an entirely different environment. This happened to me all of a sudden as I stumbled out of the countryside and wandered into the town of Saugues. Suddenly there were cars and pavements and people and shops. I was lucky not to be knocked down.

Something about Saugues struck me as cold and uninviting. Perhaps it was to do with the fact that it had clouded over and it looked like rain, or else I just wasn't ready to hit the town so soon into my journey. Either way, I was glad to put the place behind me and press on.

I had read a book years before by a Catholic priest, Father Gerald Hughes. He had written an account of his walk from Glasgow, where he was chaplain to Catholic students, to Rome. He had described how he had passed through France, going from village to village. He had found it curious that in one place everyone seemed friendly and welcoming, eager to help a traveller on his way. In another village people were grumpy and inhospitable. He just couldn't get it at first. Surely, he had wondered, France could not be made up of nice friendly villages and grumpy hostile ones? Only after a while did it dawn on him that he took his welcome with him. If he was grumpy and footsore, then the people he met would pick up on his mood and that would be the reaction he got. If he was full of joy and bonhomie, then people were invariably nice back.

I reached the hamlet of Chazeaux and began to feel some raw spots on my feet. It might have been the dampness of the previous day, the mileage and the, at times, quite rough terrain, but I was definitely feeling the first signs of blisters. Maybe that was why I'd had such a bad experience of Saugues a little earlier. I decided to call a halt for the day. It was, after all, already 3.30 in the afternoon and I had done a respectable mileage. The village had a lovely little pilgrim hostel with cascades of colourful flowers flowing everywhere, and I thought I would chance it and see if they had accommodation. On asking, the patron immediately replied, 'Yes, I will show you,' but then walked out of the house, across the square and opened the passenger door of his van.

'So where's my bed?' I asked rather sheepishly in the only way that I could dream up of dealing with this rather disconcerting turn of events.

'It is in a caravan up the road. Get in,' he ordered.

'And what about food?' I asked. 'I have none with me. Can I eat there?'

'If you want to eat, I will come for you in the evening and you can eat in the village,' was his curt reply.

'So how far is it to Le Domaine du Sauvage?' I now asked, trying to change the subject and extricate myself from a commitment to spend the night in some half-ruined caravan in the middle of nowhere (at least that was what I had convinced myself was on offer here). I had gone off the whole idea and anyway, I thought, what kind of shower can a caravan have? Not one to wash away the grime and sweat of the day.

'It is about 5.5 kilometres,' he snapped, slamming the door of the van shut.

'I think I'll keep going,' I said. 'Thank you for your help.'

'*Bon chemin*,' he replied, but I knew he didn't mean it. What he actually meant was, 'Clear off, you peasant, you have just wasted my time and I was quite happily having a nap upstairs when you turned up. You should still be walking anyway; it's only 3.30 p.m.!'

The landscape changed yet again, and it suddenly became quite 'sauvage' – no cultivation, just forest, the sort of place in which you might come face to face with the Beast of Gévaudan. It was very quiet in the woods and it was quite easy to get spooked. But I remained calm and enjoyed this woodland walk with its strange mystic silence evoked by the ancient trees all around that probably had many stories to tell.

Then the reverie was broken and I was plunged straight into the Middle Ages when three horses with riders suddenly appeared in the path right in front of me. I had not heard them coming; they were upon me all at once. They were, of course, courteous and friendly and were not carrying any weapons as far as I could see.

After that little episode, I didn't see a soul until the landscape changed abruptly yet again and I made my way across a mile or two of barren, rocky and dusty scrubland. At this point I passed a couple of clusters of pilgrims and I could see my destination up ahead. I had not phoned to book accommodation. A little pang of nervousness overtook me as I thought I had better move swiftly on to ensure my bed for the night. My feet were beginning to hurt and I knew that to go much further could be catastrophic. So I almost sprinted to Le Domaine du Sauvage and arrived to find a great huddle of, mainly, American pilgrims, checking in. It had all felt so ancient and timeless for the last few miles and now I could have been in a posh Paris hotel!

I was quite astonished by what I saw next. The caricature of the American abroad could not have fitted better, I'm afraid to say. It was obvious that the guy at the centre of this huddle was used to getting what he wanted. It was obvious also, and indeed he said it, that he was infuriated that 'these people who work here can't even speak English, how dumb is that?' As he got ever louder, some of his fellow countryfolk evidently felt distinctly uncomfortable and made 'he's not with us' noises. And he wasn't; he was with his long-suffering wife, who made it clear to me that she was very long suffering. It is amazing what people can communicate with a look! I could see the staff behind reception tensing up and trying to be as courteous as possible, but I could also see how this man's manner could so easily determine the reaction he got from others. If everyone in France was rude and unhelpful – according to him – it was no surprise since he was being so utterly obnoxious himself.

His tirade carried on into the dormitory which, unfortunately, we were assigned to share and he continued to moan about the obstinate and backward French, who didn't understand a thing about customer service. After half an hour, I realised that I either needed to start pulling his leg, thump him or walk away. I was busy tending to my now rather alarmingly raw feet and so had to listen as he lay prostrate on his bunk, his large tummy forming a perfect dome in the middle of his bed. Surprisingly, I found that Les, for that was his name, actually had a sense of humour. He was quite candid and funny about his weight problem, his rucksack problems, his problem with religion and even his problems with his wife – more eyebrow-raising from the furthest bunk. 'Les, it's about time you got your shower, honey, we'll be having dinner in half an hour.' Without pausing for breath, he went on to explain that he and his wife, Anita, from Illinois, had done the Spanish part of the walk a year before. He had lost 28 pounds in six weeks, he claimed, but had put it back on in three, which, by his calculation, made this walking lark a total waste of time. In fact, he wasn't quite sure why he was doing it all again, especially in the light of the fact that the French were so much more rude, stubborn, unhelpful and backward than the Spanish. So it went on until Les was finally coaxed into the shower by his remarkably forgiving and charming wife.

Le Domaine du Sauvage is an imposing building, the only one for miles around on a slight rise looking down over the land to the west, with the forest marking the horizon behind to the east. It was a thirteenth-century pilgrim hostel, part monastery and part castle, colossal and grand. This is probably explained by the fact that the building was founded and constructed by those warrior guardians of the pilgrim way, the Knights Templar. It is amazing to think that here we are in the twenty-first century and the atmosphere of these places is still palpable 700 years later. This is one of the real spine-tingling aspects of the Camino that I will never quite get over. For all the mobile-phone technology we have, for all the bag-carrying vehicles and the infrastructure that enables people to walk unencumbered throughout the day and still have their kit to rummage through in the evening, for all the hot and cold running water that enables modern pilgrims to arrive at the dinner table clean, refreshed and sweet-smelling, we are still part of an ancient community that goes back a thousand years. There may be no Beast of Gévaudan to assail us, no vagabonds and bandits to relieve us of our worldly goods and, sadly, no Knights Templar to rush to our aid swinging a giant saber to lop off a robber's ear and grant us another day on the journey, but the sense of continuity is palpable. It really is one of the most wonderful aspects of this ancient pilgrim way.

After a shower and having fiddled rather ineffectually with my feet, I wandered outside and met with a comical sight. A cluster of fellow pilgrims were standing around, leaning over the edge of a very ancient wall, each one of them yakking on a mobile phone. I wandered round back to the reception and ordered a pre-dinner beer (something so delightful after a day on the trail that it has to rank as one of the top five pleasures in life). I sat down at a table outside where the evening sun was offering its final, deep ochre rays and felt that, in spite of my feet, this was sheer bliss. I then whipped out my mobile phone to make a quick call to Kate and catch up on news. Not a hint of signal. It was at this point that I discovered the reason for the bizarre scene I had just witnessed. A fellow pilgrim explained to me that the only way to catch a signal was by leaning out over that ancient wall. So I went to join them after my beer and became a part of the strange ritual.

Dining at this vast auberge was quite an experience. There was no menu, or at least no choice. We were offered a pilgrim's dinner, which was €9 a head, including wine. The food was basic, plentiful and delicious, and even when our end of the table ordered more wine I noticed the price remained at €9. 'How incredibly civilised,' I said out loud, as another bottle was brought to the table.

A woman from Sweden who was walking with her Spanish husband and who lived in Valence had a wonderful way with Les, who was still mouthing off across the table. She was very direct, blunt and challenged his behaviour throughout dinner. Les, meanwhile, proceeded to eat at least three dinners, claiming that the Camino was threatening to turn him into a waif-like figure that just wouldn't suit his personality. The Swedish lady's wonderful approach somehow managed to tame this monster into a reasonably affable human being. I suppose it is like the proverbial bully: when someone stands up to them, they tend to back off and the wolf becomes a lamb.

I recounted to my new Swedish friend the disaster of my tartan trousers that I had left behind in Monistrol and, having sorted Les out, she was insistent that she could arrange on my behalf to have them delivered to me at the next auberge by one of the 'Sherpa' vehicles that ferry luggage around the Camino. It honestly felt like too much hassle and anyway, I had no idea at this stage how far I was going to get tomorrow. (It was faintly alarming that most of the other guests seemed to have their itinerary minutely worked out.) Those trousers had served me well for twenty years, surely they deserved a new life in Monistrol-d'Allier.

Meanwhile, two German women joined the conversation. Very good-humoured, they were clearly a couple and described how they had lived in a commune for more than 30 years. The conversation got quite philosophical, with lots of laughter and exchange of horror stories from the Camino: dog attacks, blisters and tendon problems that left people crawling on all fours, auberges that turned people away with the prospect of 20 kilometres to the next bed and some people that seemed to clock up absolutely colossal mileages over months and months, making the pilgrimage not so much an interlude as a way of life. As one man said, 'Once the idea of pilgrimage gets into you, it can take over your life: you never stop, never settle again.'

'Where have you walked from? I asked.

'Le Havre,' he replied nonchalantly.

It got me wondering. I had met a few people who had just started walking from their front door and all the way to Santiago. In fact, when asked – as I often have been – where the pilgrimage begins, I can't offer a definitive answer. It begins where you are; there is no official starting place. On one occasion I met a man who'd walked all the way from his home in Gothenburg. It had taken him months, and he felt as though he didn't ever want to stop.

A man called Cédric joined the conversation. What a bundle of laughs. At first, I thought he was walking with the two young women with whom he was chatting over dinner, using that forward Gallic charm that so evades us bashful Scots. It seemed like they were old friends. This was something I soon realised I had to get used to. On pilgrimage, people often strike up the most remarkable friendships within a matter of a few minutes. Cédric was a flamboyant character, with his colourful striped T-shirts, bandanas and jewellery. He was loud and ebullient and had that amazing capacity to give the impression of being able to speak several different languages – a man in his sixties with the heart (and probably libido) of a youth. I am sure I heard him speak Spanish, German and English that evening, as well as French, of course. But I realised that his command of these languages was nothing compared to his genius and passion for communication. The fact that he was pretty hopeless at English, and also equally hopeless at German according to the two German women at our table, was absolutely no barrier to his striking up instant friendships. The two young women he was with had only met him for the first time at the dinner table that evening.

CHAPTER 4
The Kindness of Strangers

The next morning, I set off from Le Domaine du Sauvage with the aim of getting to Aumont-Aubrac. Not long into the walk I came into a pine wood. With scudding clouds, a chill wind and regular soaking showers, I felt completely at home. This could have been Scotland, except that the waymarking was much better. I was rapidly coming to realise that one of the big differences between walking in Scotland and on the Camino was that almost no one was using a map. One of the guidebooks to the Chemin de St Jacques is called *Miam Miam Dodo*. It is revised every year, and it is a testimony to the way in which France has really got its act together in terms of supporting its long-distance path network. *Miam Miam Dodo* is, I think, child-speak for something like 'Yum, yum, beddy-byes'. It includes detailed information about places to eat and places to sleep, and is a meticulous guide to the route. There are a few guides to long-distance paths and pilgrim ways in Scotland, and the list is growing all the time, but not only is the infrastructure not as developed as in France, I also feel sure there is a gap in the market for a really good guide to places to stay and eat along our growing path network. There are as yet no 'pilgrim' hostels in Scotland as there are in France and Spain, but bothies could be constructed in church grounds, or else church halls could be opened up to accommodate pilgrims. Waymarking can be a bit dodgy in

Scotland too. I have twice done the St Cuthbert's Way and on both occasions have got lost at least once.

Of course, for some, navigation is part of the joy of walking. Certainly, on the route through France, all the way back to the Middle Ages, signs and stone crosses marked the pilgrim way. In the Middle Ages maps were rare and valuable items, and could be wildly inaccurate. It is only really since the nineteenth century and the development of accurate surveying techniques that they have been reliable guides for the traveller. No doubt seasoned pilgrims would have shared their experiences with others about to set off, and intending pilgrims would have a story in their head about what to expect. It is also interesting to speculate whether an illiterate medieval pilgrim would have been any the wiser with a map in their hand anyway. A mixture of stories, rather like the Aboriginal Song Lines, and these stone crosses would have had to do along a well-trodden and well-populated path.

Pilgrim routes lead us to places with wonderful stories to share. The Rev. Alexander John Forsyth, parish minister of Belhelvie in Aberdeenshire in the early nineteenth century, was a keen field sportsman but was unhappy with the firing mechanism of his rifle. He had to fill it with gunpowder that invariably got damp, so he invented the first percussion mechanism to be used in a firearm and had great fun trying to sell his idea to the British Army. When they dropped the idea, he is supposed to have tried to negotiate with Napoleon Bonaparte. His would be a great story to tell on a pilgrimage route through the North-east, putting Belhelvie on the map.

The parish of Fortingall in Perthshire has one of the oldest trees in Europe and is reputed to be the birthplace of Pontius Pilate. The parish of Luss on Loch Lomondside, where the Celtic evangelist St Kessog did so much to spread the Gospel and then was executed by Druids, is a beautiful spot and already has a 'Pilgrim Palace', constructed from surplus Royal Navy portacabins. I can't help but think that there is a real opportunity for congregations all over Scotland to revive their sometimes flagging spirits by sharing their amazing stories about faith and the rich cultural narrative of their nation.

I have already described my meeting with Jacques at La Ferme du Barry in Aumont-Aubrac that night. What felt like an instant friendship emerged over a single evening, only to disappear the following day as our journeys went their separate ways. I found myself reflecting on the people I had met along the route, and my thoughts turned to a newspaper article I had read recently, written by the Edinburgh author Alexander McCall Smith, in which he had explored the nature of friendship. I have always liked him as a writer and have admired his desire to see the good in people. I have a couple of reasons to be grateful to him personally too. But on the Camino I found that our views on friendship were beginning to differ. The article had a very 'Edinburgh' take on the whole concept. He suggested that it might take years to establish a real friendship and that before being in a position properly to invest in a friendship one had to go through many preliminaries. I have to say that on the Camino I was meeting people that I could quite confidently call friends, even if our acquaintance only lasted a matter of hours.

I have often felt that when I meet someone, I can, very frequently, tell if this is someone whom I would like to get to know within an instant. Friendships, I think, don't always have to be tried and tested or last a lifetime. They can spontaneously arise, and then you move on, but you are the richer for having been open enough, made yourself vulnerable enough and been frank enough to have made a connection, an exchange of humanity.

Indeed, I think that one of the things that our settled urban life often prevents us from doing is really engaging with our neighbours. We fear that if we disclose too much we might be put into an awkward situation, and, having given too much of ourselves away the other person might have something 'on us' to use against us in the future, so we hold back. The freedom and trust of the Camino allows real friendship to arise and develop very quickly and can be a genuine source of blessing, even if it does not last longer than a few miles or a pilgrim dinner. There is a biblical imperative to be open to the blessing of the empty-handed stranger, the unknown one who just might be Christ in disguise. Just think of the disciples on the road to Emmaus (Luke 24) and how, when they broke bread with a perfect stranger and offered hospitality in open friendship, their hearts burned within them as they felt they had met their friend Jesus whom they'd seen die on the Cross just days before. There is an old Celtic rune of hospitality I love, which concludes, 'Often, often, often, comes Christ in the stranger's guise.' And, of course, the writer of the Epistle to the Hebrews invites his readers to make hospitality to strangers a special care, for 'thereby some have entertained angels unawares' (Hebrews 13:2).

After the mass in the church, which I described in the Prologue, and after parting from Jacques, I returned to wait for my transport to the convent down the road, when another interesting encounter took place.

The Carmelite monks came back to La Ferme for their breakfast and we got chatting. It was an opportunity to test the ground and see whether they would be horrified that they had served communion to a Protestant. Of course, they were not horrified at all. In fact they were delighted. I knew from reading Robert Louis Stevenson's account of his journey in this region that this had been something of a Protestant stronghold and that just as Scotland had a bloody and none-too-proud past of religious intolerance and fanaticism, so also there had been much bloodshed and rancour around the Catholic–Protestant divide here. Further back in history, the Cathars had been all but wiped out for their beliefs, too. But there was not a trace of suspicion in these Carmelites, just a fresh-faced, youthful warmth.

I get a strong feeling, and it is one I certainly got from Halo and Hannah, that we are in a 'post-Christian' world. People carry around in their heads their ideas about the universe, in their hearts many carry the message of Jesus and are deeply committed to the spiritual search. They have an awareness in their hearts of the essence of the Spirit of Life, a deep connectedness to the universe. Frequently, however, it is the churchy language that we have used to define these things that puts people off.

The agony, inconvenience and setback I was suffering at the end of only day three was actually a blessing. I learned important lessons, not just about Camino life, but life in general. Jacques was able to engage in his vocation to care for a weary pilgrim's feet and taught me much. He revived my sagging spirits by enabling me to feel useful in ministering back to him. I accepted help. I listened to people like Halo, who said it was important to be able to stop, to slow down, to put limits on ourselves and take the pressure off, or else we would do harm to ourselves.

I now see that what Halo was referring to was not just my present physical condition but the condition of the world. We go so fast, we consume so much, we never slow down, and we are slowly and steadily consuming the world. The Camino is a metaphor for so many aspects of life. How often have I preached about slowing down, caring for ourselves and taking time to take stock but never taken my own advice? I had been putting myself under silly and unsustainable pressure for three days, and on this journey I had rendered myself almost completely useless. Maybe I'd been doing that for 30 years? It was with these thoughts that I boarded the minibus that took me onward to the Couvent de Malet at Saint-Côme-d'Olt. I had arranged to stay there for two nights as a chance to stop, to switch off, to heal if possible, and to reflect. I wasn't at all sure how I would pass the time off the road, but maybe that was exactly as it should be for now.

CHAPTER 5

Get Thee to a Nunnery

As the minibus trundled through a section of the French countryside that looked very like Scotland, I felt a little sheepish and like a cheat. I knew that I couldn't realistically walk the whole way through France to the Spanish border and get to Santiago in the time I had given myself, but it felt that I shouldn't be reduced to this so early on. In addition, the landscape, a wide, windswept plateau of heather moorland felt so familiar, I really wanted to be out there and walking in it. But soon we began a descent through beautiful picturesque woodlands and eventually reached the Lot valley and the convent of the Angels of Mercy at Saint-Côme-d'Olt. Olt is the old Occitan name for the River Lot. As I had arrived at around 1 p.m., all was quiet with no one around; all the real pilgrims were on the move. The reception didn't open until four, so I sat in the grounds brooding and muttering to myself, limping around the place whenever I got too chilly – it could get surprisingly cold when the sun was hidden by cloud.

When eventually they let me in, I was given a small but delightful single room. It felt like a real place of retreat. There was a glorious view out to woods where cattle munched contentedly and life went on at a quiet, sedate pace all around. It is a very odd feeling to come to terms with the idea of not going anywhere for a few days. For now, I decided I was too lame, too tender even, to venture the mile down to the village to have a wander around there. Instead, I flung open my windows and breathed in the air and decided that this too must be seen as a gift. It was a beautiful clean room – it even had en-suite facilities – and, in this vast building, I was left alone. There were very few people about. I lay down on my bed and pulled out my novel. I had brought one book to read in addition to my guidebooks but had started to resent the extra weight that this big novel added and reflected that, anyway, there had been very little time to sit around reading so far. I hadn't had a moment to open it. So this would be my reading time, part of my recuperation.

I lay down to read and hardly paused until the novel was finished. I let my feet air, I rubbed my strained ankle with some herbal cream that a chemist had recommended and did almost nothing else except dutifully hobbling downstairs at the summons of the bell to worship in the chapel and eat in the refectory. There were perhaps ten Ursuline nuns, and they warbled their way through the services, none of them very noticeably taking any leading role in the liturgy and none with any obvious musical talent. Leading the liturgy was a task they would leave to a priest who would turn up every now and then to say mass. I wondered how it must feel for these women to be observing this ancient liturgy – probably they knew it word for word – but not to be able to be fully involved unless the priest came to take the place of Christ. For a Presbyterian interested in the notions of the motherhood of God and the sacred feminine, all this felt so backward and limiting, and so demeaning of the place of women. But I had learned from my mother, a highly opinionated woman none the less, that you should never judge.

It still made me mad that no woman who menstruated could be allowed near the blood of Christ. How on earth had such nonsense crept into the community of the Nazarene peasant, Jesus, who counted amongst his closest friends many women, including those whom the culture of Jesus's day had excluded?

There was a small group of pilgrims at each meal. A familiar face from Aumont-Aubrac turned up. It was Patrick from Toulouse, who had promised to come pilgrimage walking in Scotland one day. It was nice to see him again, but the entire setting and atmosphere of the convent was in such contrast to the ebullience of La Ferme du Barry that there wasn't quite the same bonhomie as there had been a couple of nights before. It was probably down to the absence of alcohol here as much as the ambience.

The rest of the time, I simply brooded, communicated with Kate, and enjoyed a few hilarious moments such as the one when I discussed at great length the spelling of the password for the Wi-Fi system with an ancient and gloriously bossy nun. And then, in a solemn ceremony, I added Victoria Hislop's absorbing book about Thessaloniki, *The Thread*, to the convent library, full as it was with devotional literature on how to be a good Catholic. I placed it next to a copy of Augustine's *Confessions*.

In the midst of this great 'transhumance', this river of people on the march, I was immobilised by my own stupidity and not a part of this migration, at least for the moment. I felt feeble, and it was such a big lesson to learn that this feeling of frailty made me quite so uncomfortable. Oddly enough, the few people I had communicated with over the last few days about my plight had been hugely generous, understanding and sympathetic. I may have felt as though I had fallen and been humbled, but the people I was meeting saw none of the sense of failure that I felt in myself; all they wanted to do was offer kindness and understanding. How frequently the feelings we have about ourselves diverge from the thoughts we imagine others are having about us. As I read once, sometimes the last thing we learn about ourselves is our effect on others, and one of the things we frequently fail to work out is just what others are really thinking of us.

Perhaps tomorrow, I thought, now that I had finished my book, I could start writing my letters. I had planned to write at least fifty of them to people back home. I felt it important to share my experience with those who had made it all possible. But what would I say? What would I tell them? Would I confess to having been a fool and overdoing it and to lying low in a convent for two days reading a book? What would they think? Why did it matter so much what people thought?

CHAPTER 6
The Rule of Resonance

My two days of respite at Saint-Côme-d'Olt had not quite rendered me fully fit, but I knew I was ready to move on. I walked on through the village, which is made up almost entirely of medieval houses. The church in the centre has the most wonderful twisted spire, just like Chesterfield. For part of the day, I walked along the banks of the River Lot, a lovely gentle stream with cattle standing up to their haunches looking for all the world like aurochs, the wild ancient cattle of Europe from which all our domestic ones are bred. At the end of a more modest day of walking, I arrived at the most idyllic of places, St-Pierre-de-Bessuéjouls, a converted monastery about three or four kilometres along the Lot valley from Espalion.

The busy town of Espalion is not mentioned in my guidebook, but it does get an honourable mention in *Miam Miam Dodo*. On the way there, I had taken a detour up to the Vierge de Vermus, where there is a stunning view across the Lot valley and a very fine statue of the Blessed Virgin Mary. I had been really struck by the timelessness of all I had seen on my journey. The cattle, the stone crosses, the statues of the Blessed Virgin Mary and the gorgeous chapels and churches that pepper the route all the way to Santiago, and the ancient asphalt-free paths all gave a sense that the modern world had bypassed this region of France. Espalion temporarily broke a spell.

Everything was about to change that night as one of my dearest and oldest friends, Jon, was due to arrive from Norway to walk with me for a few days. I'd had the idea that we might meet up in Espalion, but it was really quite a disappointing place. There were some nice buildings but lots of ugly ones too, and too much of the twenty-first century intruded into the medieval calm of the Camino. I arrived at the main church in town just as the congregation (a healthy crowd) were leaving after the morning service. Another smaller crowd, all smartly dressed, were arriving for what looked like a baby's baptism. A friendly person wondered if I'd like to stay. In my pilgrim gear, I decided that I looked too shabby and that my presence would lower the tone considerably. So I beat a hasty retreat out of the church and out of town.

St-Pierre-de-Bessuéjouls restored the sense of inhabiting a medieval world. Sitting in the sun in the courtyard I could sense my wounds were healing. My feet were toughening up little by little, and the herbal cream that I was rubbing on my ankle seemed to be working. I phoned Jon and told him where I was. It all seemed rather comical that he was in Oslo about to board a plane for Paris and that he'd be able to home in on this tiny little place at some point in the course of that evening. It seemed impossible, but we'd give it a try.

As I sat there, I reread an article that my friend Jo had given me just before I left entitled 'Rites of way: behind the pilgrimage revival' from the *Guardian Review*, 15 June 2012 by Robert Macfarlane. I had just read his very fine book *The Old Ways* and in the article he refers to Václav Cílek, who talked of a 'Rule of Resonance' for the pilgrim: 'A smaller place with which we resonate is more important than a place of great pilgrimage.' St-Pierre-de-Bessuéjouls felt just like that, a small gem of a place which had captivated me as soon as I arrived. I had been thinking a lot about Santiago, the ultimate destination of my walk, and I was now certain of its almost complete irrelevance but for being the place where my journey home might begin. The smaller place of deep resonance was this and my hosts Gilles and Françoise Sanglier. They had made me so welcome. The place was a beautiful former monastery set in the most wonderful hamlet. It had been painstakingly and tastefully restored, and was cared for lovingly. I was the only pilgrim staying that night, and they entertained me to dinner as a family friend.

Over a wonderful meal they shared their story of how a few years ago they had walked the Camino together. At that time Françoise had been involved with breeding Shetland ponies and Gilles was a financier in Paris. They had stayed in this gîte themselves and had fallen in love with the magic of this spot. A few months after their return from Galicia, they noticed that the gîte had come up for sale. It was too much of a providential sign, so they bought the place, gave up their jobs and hadn't looked back.

They had prepared one of those simple but delicious meals that I love so much. It began with an aperitif of rosé wine mixed with grape syrup, remarkably refreshing, a sort of rural cocktail, according to Françoise. This was followed by vegetarian pâté made from lentil and carrot, and then we had chicken with mozzarella cheese and spicy sauce on a bed of deliciously seasoned rice, then some cheese – a single wedge of heavenly 'mountain' Comté. The flowers in the high pasture where the cattle graze in summer add a distinctive and unsurpassed flavour to it. All was finished off with a small apple crumble. It was washed down with a carafe of some exquisite local red wine. It sounds like a lot of food, but the portions were elegant and sufficient, so by the end of the meal I felt wonderfully nourished but in no sense overfed or bloated. They clearly loved this new life and told me that 98 per cent of all the people they had to stay either in the gîte or in the pilgrim bunkhouse were delightful. The mind boggles to think what the other 2 per cent might have been like.

Françoise described how she too had been keen on walking in the mountains but her perspective had changed when she started on these sacred journeys prompted by her father, who at the age of 80 had introduced her to her first pilgrimage walk. I went off to bed at ten, hugely satisfied and feeling much better about life. Gilles had been a great help with regard to Jon's arrival and had arranged for a taxi driver he knew to meet Jon off a train in Rodez and bring him straight here. We thought it might be one in the morning before he arrived.

Waking from my vivid dreams a few hours later, it took me a few moments to remember where I was, and I lay in bed thinking about the life of this old monastery which had lost its last monk in the 1950s. As I lay there I reflected on some of the things I had read earlier in Macfarlane's *Guardian* article. Macfarlane quoted Rowan Williams, always to be relied on for deep insight, who had written of the recent revival of interest in pilgrimage that 'a whole generation of new pilgrims [was emerging], wishing to cut through the clutter of institutions and achieve self-discovery in a new place'. That certainly chimed with my understanding. Institutional life in the church has sometimes got bogged down in telling people what to think and what to believe, leaving no space for the joy of discovery. In so many places the church has become an anxious institution, obsessed with its own self-preservation and nostalgic for a lost golden age. But here on the journey of the pilgrim, people just set off, not being sure, not being fettered by institutional boundaries, journeying with hope and even being prepared to get a little lost. Isn't this, I was beginning to think, a much more helpful approach to encounter mystery than the proscribed, dogmatic structure of institutions that often operate in a way that no longer makes sense to so many people?

And this experience of walking through France on pilgrimage was remarkable for another reason. Robert Macfarlane had suggested in his article that walking on ancient routes offered a kind of antidote to the structures of our society that have been 'privatised or made over to capital'. Certainly, there was commerce and trade on the Camino. Gilles and Françoise were eking out a living offering hospitality to pilgrims. There were cafés and restaurants with reduced-rate pilgrim menus, there were shops selling the odd bit of pilgrim paraphernalia, there were minivans ferrying rucksacks and the odd weary pilgrim about the countryside, but there was a total absence of any corporate intrusion into the whole Camino experience. No big companies had found a way to franchise the pilgrim operation. It was refreshing to notice the absence of those signs of the corporate takeover that seem to dominate the modern world. Pilgrimage, says Macfarlane, is a 'wonder voyage out of the verifiable into the marvellous'. Amen to that.

As I lay there all these thoughts swooped around my semi-conscious mind like swifts on a summer's day, screeching their significance as they flitted in and out. And in the midst of this pleasant reverie a twenty-first-century sound intruded into my hearing. It was strange and disconcerting at first; it was the sound of a car drawing up, doors being banged, quiet talk, a thank you and greetings. I saw it was 1.20 a.m. and Jon had arrived. A miracle!

How wonderful it was to see him and how remarkable that he had found his way to this little place of medieval tranquillity. But here he was, and for the next three days I would have a companion, a friend to complain to about the state of my feet. It would be a special opportunity to chat and catch up with a dear friend I'd known since we were both students in Edinburgh sharing a flat in the early 1980s. It was just what I needed at that moment of fragility. We spent a short while saying hello and laughing together at this incongruous meeting, but soon Jon had got himself installed in a bed across the dormitory and we dozed off.

CHAPTER 7
Bread-sharer for the Journey

We ate a frugal breakfast together at 7 a.m., I introduced Jon to Françoise and Gilles, and then we were off. After about an hour my feet, which were fiery and raw, began to settle a little, but my ankle was still swollen and tender. At the first opportunity in the astounding fortified village of Estaing, I bought some painkillers. The young girl in the pharmacy suggested that some strapping would be a good idea for my ankle too, so I bought a very nifty little black sock that bound itself tightly around the tender area. Like so many of the villages here, Estaing seemed almost entirely medieval, and the boulangerie, which, disappointingly, was shut, looked as though it had been closed at the time of the French Revolution and had never reopened. I had a little bread, cheese and sausage left over from previous days, and Jon had some sandwiches, so later on we sat at the roadside and had a hilarious lunch, which seemed to shock some of the cattle in the adjacent field, as Jon pretended to be a strange Nordic benefactor extolling the health-giving properties of Norwegian venison sandwiches. Just like old times, my madcap friend from Norway brought a wonderful sense of the ridiculous to the proceedings and we laughed uproariously at almost nothing. It was good to be together.

In the afternoon we walked through some quite magnificent countryside, ancient field patterns bordered by heroic oak trees of indeterminate age, paths that gave the impression of having been in use for hundreds of years. There was a succession of curious buildings in the middle of fields that could have been shepherds' bothies, dovecots or communal bread ovens; I guess we saw all three.

It was still a well-populated region, and it reminded me of the vastness of France. Graham Robb, in his magnificent book *The Discovery of France*, describes how, until the advent of the canal system and the railways soon after, France had the feel of a continent, every region remote and the whole place quite ungovernable. He describes how, during the Napoleonic period, a ploy to keep control of the nation had been to map it. He tells of how a cartographer turned up in one village and set up his apparatus only to be executed by the locals as an evil sorcerer, as they thought his strange equipment was a device for summoning up the devil. France was divided into many distinct regions and languages and, though dominated by Paris, he reckons that right up until the 1870s anything up to 80 per cent of the population had no understanding of Parisian French, the language that now dominates the entire country.

One of the strange parallels between France and Scotland is the fact that until quite recently a child might be punished at a Breton school for speaking the language of his forefathers, just as some young people in Scotland were beaten for using Gaelic or Scots in the school playground. The sad truth is that the church colluded in this cultural persecution, disdaining not only indigenous language but also culture. France certainly is a vast country, and though the countryside remains healthily populated, there are many derelict and abandoned properties. Another thing we noticed was the very large amount of ancient farm machinery, especially rusting old tractors that stood around almost every farmyard. Jon deduced that much of this machinery had probably appeared in the aftermath of the Second World War, as the Americans sought to inject new life into the shattered economies of Europe through the Marshall Plan.

We spent that night at a small gîte called l'Orée du Chemin in a hamlet called Massip. A pleasant enough place. It was a walk that day of something like 22 kilometres and I felt that I was coping, although I am sure I was making a big fuss most of the time. But Jon has a wonderful way of just being there with kindness, support and understanding as well as a little playful bossiness, which never goes amiss when the intention behind it is sincere. We descended into the bowels of the gîte for dinner, conjured up for us by a lady who appeared from along the road. She turned out to be a local farmer's wife; this was a sideline job for her, a source of a little extra revenue on the farm. And what a sublime meal she prepared. The stew was beef, deliciously tender with a melt-in-the-mouth consistency, and the array of fresh herbs simply dazzled the palate. A bowl of peas and carrots, obviously freshly picked and podded and again blended with aromatic herbs and butter, added so much to our meal, and the delightful waxy potatoes tasted as though they had been growing just a few hours before, which was probably the case. Naturally, all of it was accompanied by a delicious, fruity red wine, spicy but smooth, and what a delight not to wince at the prospect of paying for another bottle – however much wine was needed was brought to the table with a generous, understanding smile. They clearly knew the thirst of the pilgrim.

The company was a mixed bag that evening, and all the conversation was in French. A rather loud and self-important man from Geneva interrogated us all and announced that his job was to paint shutters. Apparently this is an expression for someone who is retired but keeping busy. Our other friend spoke in very precise French and I was able to follow nearly everything he said. Our Genevan companion began to ask around the table what was motivating us all to do the pilgrimage. Was it a spiritual or religious thing or were we just keen walkers? I managed to blunder through a few inarticulate thoughts about the spiritual dimension to my journey without sounding too 'churchy', I hope. Another attempt to underplay anything that might be interpreted as piety. The conversation was very masculine, with comments about daily mileage done, about how many other *grandes randonnées* had been accomplished and a few reflections about kit. The whole atmosphere had become somewhat competitive and loud as the wine flowed and tongues were loosened.

Then a quiet, unassuming French lady who had said almost nothing during the whole course of the dinner was homed in on by the Genevan. Following a momentary lull in the macho conversation, he turned to her and asked her why she was walking the Chemin de St Jacques. Her answer was very simple and modest: she was walking to give thanks. It was, of course, the perfect answer. There was no need for her to elaborate; her few words were a gift, if not a gentle rebuke, to the rest of us. That is, of course, a huge part of the pilgrim experience: just to be in a position to do this, to have the freedom, the space and the time to walk and to reflect on life as a gift. The only response is gratitude.

Back in our dormitory, the man from Geneva set a pattern that I was destined to become all too familiar with over the coming weeks. He was quite portly and lay down to sleep lying flat on his back. Dropping off almost immediately, he then began to snore with a remarkable force that meant the rest of us didn't stand a chance of nodding off ourselves. In his inimitable style, Jon had spotted that there was a spare bed on the landing. Fortunately, I was able to constrain him just as he approached our Genevan fellow traveller to shake him awake and order him to the corridor. 'Jon, you can't do that,' I interceded. But as the night wore on I began to wish I hadn't stopped him. Instead of sending him out to the landing, Jon went himself. I stayed on in the dormitory, inserted my earplugs and tried to doze off, but the plugs only annoyed me and didn't do a thing to reduce the volume of the steady, regular apocalypse of his snoring.

I am amazed that we don't hear more stories of irate, sleep-starved pilgrims assassinating their fellows in the night as they are reduced to hysteria by stentorian snoring (and promiscuous flatulence). In an act of quite remarkable forbearance, the unassuming French lady appeared to sleep through the entire night and left in complete silence in the morning, almost unnoticed, like mist lifting off a meadow.

CHAPTER 8

Journey to Middle-earth

The next morning, we did our best to find Golinhac, but this scattered and quite eerily dead little settlement had no medieval heart that we could discern. Probably we didn't hunt it down with enough endeavour; it just seemed to be a place with empty but pristine holiday houses. Everyone had gone home to Paris at the end of the summer holidays. So we moved swiftly on and found ourselves at Espeyrac, where, thanks to Jon's bossiness, I posted home my hateful leather hat and a few other items I now realised I wouldn't need. I spent €28 sending that stupid hat home. I should have given it to the curious bull that was eyeing it up in the adjacent field.

We had another coffee and bought some food for lunch. After lunch, the landscape began to change and we left this pleasant agricultural terrain and began a steady descent into thick, ancient oak forest. What seemed bizarre here was that the agriculture took place on the tops of the hills and the forest filled the valleys down below. You'd expect it to be the other way about. These forests were a delight, and once again it felt like a journey back in time. I could imagine one of the Knights Templar charging out of the woods at any moment, just to check we were okay and hadn't been set upon by bandits. And then we stumbled into the small town in which we'd decided to spend the night. I had read about this place in the guidebook, and we had agreed to try to find a hotel and have a good meal in a restaurant. Its name was Conques.

Nothing in the guidebook prepared us for what we found here in this lost city in the woods. It clings precariously to the hillside, the great twin spires of the cathedral soaring above the trees. We felt we had arrived in Middle-earth. The ancient lane by which we entered the town gave the impression of a place with no proper roads and consequently no traffic. But of course there were roads here and, as in every historic French town, there were a few cars in the centre. Indeed, it seems to me to be a popular French pastime to try to get your car down the narrowest of roads and to park it in the prettiest historic squares for no other reason than to dispel the magical illusion of the pilgrim or the tourist that one really has travelled back in time.

Conques completely blew us away. It has a charm and richness that is quite unique. I don't suppose there has been a new house built here for 400 years. As we entered the town we did, however, come across a very discreetly positioned tourist hotel. As we passed it a great crowd lined the road and burst into a round of spontaneous applause, cheering us and congratulating us as hardy pilgrims who had chosen to walk rather than take the bus. It was a nice gesture. Just off the main square we walked into the Auberge St Jacques and booked the last room in the place. It's always difficult to avoid looking a bit guilty when another pair of weary pilgrims turns up hard on your heels and gets turned away.

The cathedral of St Foy dates from the eleventh century, and it is a stunning place. In the evening, following a shower and a couple of beers, we spent a while in the building and suddenly realised that we were quite alone. I don't know what possessed me but I began to sing, quite loudly, the hymn 'Veni Creator Spiritus', a ninth-century plainsong chant. It actually sounded quite good in the acoustic and Jon was impressed. It felt like our little offering of thanksgiving. I was pulling through my dark tunnel. The company, the help, the laughter, the applause even and the sheer wonder of the places we were walking through were all bringing about healing and restoring my soul. As Hilaire Belloc wrote, 'The volume, depth and intensity of the world is something that only those on foot will ever experience.'

It was walking that had got me into a mess early on, setting off too fast, ill-prepared and with sodden feet. But it was walking through this wonderful countryside, in such good company, that had provided the healing I needed. The magic of the landscape, the sense of profound connection to past generations and the fact that this town itself and its remarkable cathedral owed its whole existence to the Camino all added to the sense of being caught up in an endeavour that was not a solitary initiative of mine but one that had its origins way back in time and that had caught hold of millions before me. We were part of a community of people seeking connection to the great mystery, hoping for change and transformation through walking and sharing a journey that may have begun in the ninth century, when the Bishop of Le Puy-en-Velay set off to Santiago.

The astronauts on Apollo 8, who first orbited the moon and watched the earth rise on its far side, were quite overcome by the wonder and glory of the blue-green gem that is our planet spinning silently in the vast blackness of space. It was an epiphany, a rediscovery of a familiar place that was being seen from a different perspective for the first time. James Lovelock, the British scientist who dreamt up the theory of Gaia – the earth as a single, self-sustaining organic system – suggested that we started the space race with the intention of exploring outer space and in the process rediscovered the earth. As I walked through this beautiful country, a land full of ancient stories, natural beauty and man-made wonders, the world was slowly being re-enchanted for me, and I was finding a renewed sense of belonging to the earth community in a way that was quite unexpected. My individuality was being subsumed into a commonality of time as well as place, and I was beginning to wonder if the biggest deception of history is the idea of the individual self. I was rediscovering the earth, or it was reclaiming me, and it was lighting up my life and healing me.

Just as the landscape was re-enchanting me, I reflected on how sometimes the church has been for many a source of disenchantment. I began to feel the truth of that and not a little uneasy about the radical individualism that has taken hold of our religion, our politics and the sense of our own humanity in Western thought through the years. The perspective that often runs through Western Christianity is that the Divine seeks out individual souls and that faith is a matter of choice. This pilgrimage, catching us up in a journeying community walking through the landscape, was undermining this perspective. The Camino was asserting its pull over us.

Dinner on the balcony at the hotel was sheer pleasure. We had not yet passed out of the region in which *aligot* is a speciality, so I was able to introduce Jon to it. Delicious as it was, it wasn't a patch on La Ferme du Barry. But after good food, good wine and good chat, it was time for a night of contented, dream-filled sleep.

CHAPTER 9
The Coupar Angus of France

My dream was completely medieval, so the sound that woke me at about 5.30 was a cause of alarm and confusion. It was the bread van delivering our breakfast – astoundingly fresh croissants. We headed out of Conques as the mist still clung to the trees in this mystical valley. Just outside the village is a chapel that looks back up to the cathedral of St Foy, or St Faith, a third-century martyr who'd been burned to death during Diocletian's persecution of the Christians for refusing to make a pagan sacrifice. Her bones were brought to Conques by a monk who apparently stole them from their resting place at Agen. I suppose he wanted to put his village on the map and he certainly succeeded. The place has been a pilgrimage destination for a thousand years for those wanting to make it to Santiago or visit the shrine of St Foy.

At the little chapel below the city you get a tremendous view back to Conques, and the whole place looks utterly magical. The chapel was constructed over a spring, where apparently miraculous healings of eye problems had been reported. Indeed, St Foy was famous during her life for her ability to cure eye disorders. We splashed some water into our eyes in the vain hope that our accelerating, post-50-year-old long-sightedness might be slowed down a little. We will see.

At the top of the hill we emerged out of the woods onto a heather moor, and a little further on reached the agricultural world that inhabits the hilltops. It felt as though Conques were a forgotten place deep in inner earth where time had stood still and life operated in a quite different way, apart from the regular visit of the bread van. We chose a slightly longer but more interesting-looking route. I had another episode of leaving my stick behind following a stop in Noailhac. Jon in his kindness sprinted back to retrieve it and we were off again, marching on to Decazeville. This was the biggest town I'd seen in over a week, too big to contemplate staying in, so we headed on a few kilometres further.

We crossed the River Lot again to Livinhac-le-Haut and found our gîte up a little lane. It was clean but sparse with a rather bossy lady in charge. Jon disappeared off to take a phone call as our host gave a sermon on dos and don'ts: don't put your bags on the floor, use the mats provided, no noise after 10 p.m., wash round the shower after use, no dirty boots anywhere near the building and, since there was a washing line in a garden some distance away, no washing was to be hung up in or around the house. Jon might have thought he'd got away with it by disappearing off, but I listened from upstairs in the dormitory as the lady repeated her speech word for word for his benefit when he finally re-emerged.

We got cleaned up and set off to explore Livinhac. The only way I can describe it is that it is the Coupar Angus of France. Now, if you don't know Coupar Angus, I intend what I'm about to say with the utmost genuine affection. Coupar Angus is an ancient rural town in the heart of Strathmore in Scotland. It has the feel of an ancient place that is charmingly crumbly and a little rough round the edges. When I lived nearby I loved it for its gritty, slightly scruffy charm. Armies of oddly dressed chicken-factory workers stood in huddles after their shifts, giving the place an incongruous feel of a town half rural and half industrial. Livinhac had a similar feel.

We visited a bar at the top of Livinhac in the main square. I guess it was the time of year but the wasps were out in force and there was not much to commend the place as a pre-dinner hang-out. The question of where to eat dinner also began to exercise us. A helpful man from St Malo walking with two female friends we'd passed several times in the course of the day suggested we might find somewhere good at the campsite down by the river.

We made our way down there, passing a little shop where a young man was busy painting a wall. It looked as though he was soon to open a restaurant, and we thought it was a pity that it was still a work in progress as it all looked quite charming. We headed on to the river and the campsite. The bar was in a marquee and there were no campers about. The holiday season was clearly at an end. It did not feel particularly promising, actually quite edgy, if anything. As the bartender gruffly poured us two beers and slapped them down with a huffy, threatening scowl, Jon succumbed to one of his bouts of uncontrollable laughter, which invariably happen in moments of awkwardness and uncertainty.

The prospect of a microwaved pizza or a strangled chicken for supper seemed to be getting ever nearer. The day was saved by our St Malo friends who had turned up not far behind us, clearly on a similar search. They read the situation exactly and indicated that the man at the wee shop in the village wasn't opening a restaurant as such but would nonetheless feed a maximum of five people if we happened to show up at about 8 p.m. looking suitably hungry. So we clubbed together and made our way back up to the village, and with great relief were welcomed into this little place where the owner told us he offered food only to those he liked the look of, didn't charge, but asked for a donation and expected us to help with the washing up.

It turned out that our host was an Italian, Sandro. He'd been on pilgrimage himself, and was still on it, even though for the time being he wasn't doing any walking. He was on a journey to a different world and was committed to try and bring it about. He'd teamed up with a fellow pilgrim and they'd decided to settle in Livinhac. He was evangelical about the alternative economy and radical culture of the Camino and how it could reconfigure the world. Life is about hospitality, he told us, and by offering it you get good things back. There is no need to insert a commercial transaction between the host and the guest, no need to put a price on everything. Indeed, that was half of the problem with the world, that everything was now being measured only by its monetary value. His take on life was that generosity and openness always repay us richly.

It reminded me of something St Paul said in one of his letters: 'You will always be rich enough to be generous' (2 Corinthians 9:11). If you flip this statement around, then if you are greedy and acquisitive you might well end up denying yourself the good things that you need or desire. It is our anxious grasping after more and more that is destroying the people and the world around us. In our insatiable desire for more and our anxiety about not having enough we are blighting our world, plundering the resources of the planet and making the life of the poorest, who are always the most vulnerable, ever more wretched. In doing this the wealth, comfort and security that we desire for ourselves becomes harder to achieve.

Sandro was a radical voice, a prophetic figure trying to live out an alternative life that subverts the 'god horizon' of commerce and corporatism, where those with power and money tell us that their way is the only way in which humanity can operate. Some would call the present arrangement of free-market capitalism the suicide economy. You could dismiss Sandro as loopy and a romantic idealist, but I think he may well have a point.

Sandro made us all pizza, and copious amounts of it. We chatted, laughed, philosophised and had a wonderfully enlightening and magical evening, the whole thing yet another moment full of rich things to ponder. Then we helped with the washing up and, of course, made our monetary donation to defray his costs. And at the end of the evening Sandro gave us his own version of a Camino stamp. He rubbed a felt pen over his big toe and pressed it onto our *créanciales*, writing underneath, '*La vita è bella.*' It certainly was. Apart from an aching ankle, my feet were definitely on the mend now, and Jon and I returned to our gîte with the prospect of a walk to Figeac the next day – the last day of our time walking together.

CHAPTER 10

The Interior Pilgrimage

We set off in bright sunshine for Figeac. The day became hot but we covered the 25 kilometres in good time. Jon had spent part of each day on his phone dealing with the day-to-day issues of his job as an architect back in Oslo. He had taken a few days off work to join me, but he had not been able entirely to leave his work behind. For me, this was part of the privilege and discipline of pilgrimage – to find yourself cut free from the ties, duties, appointments and deadlines by which we live our lives day in, day out. It is remarkable what happens to your mind when you create this kind of space. Both on the move and in my two-day stop at Saint-Côme-d'Olt, I found myself becoming quite alarmingly empty-headed. I had set off on this pilgrimage with ideas about how I might fill my days. I would plan this, give some thought to that, strategise about some things and review the situation of my working life. The last ten years had been an exciting period of developing new initiatives, both in the church and with the foundation of the Grassmarket Community Project. Our long-cherished ambition of creating a new building to house this work had come to fruition and the new building was about to open soon after my return. I had reached a plateau and it was a good moment to take stock. So the pilgrimage had come at a wonderful time. The trouble was, I often wasn't thinking about very much at all.

I reflected on this. I remember when I began my work on my final project to complete the Doctor of Ministry course. At one point, just before writing up our dissertation, I had confessed to my tutor that I was confused about what to write. He had replied, 'Don't worry. Stay confused.' It was an odd bit of advice at the time, but I saw eventually what he meant. If I had got my ideas sorted out too quickly, I would not have absorbed any new thinking or assimilated any fresh insight. There is a sort of confusion and chaos, numbness even, that is a requirement for fresh thinking. I certainly feel that the final project I eventually wrote has gone on shaping and feeding me theologically as a minister.

It all clicked into place one day when a fellow Doctor of Ministry candidate declared that all the ministry experience reports that I was writing (these are accounts of the practice of ministry that go to the heart of your concern in the context in which you work) were about strangers. He was right. In the particular place I was ministering at the time, St Machar's Cathedral in Old Aberdeen, a huge part of my ministry, time and effort was being deployed in attending to people who had no affiliation to the church but wanted things from me. It might be a homeless person begging and badgering for a handout. It might be one of the local heroin addicts looking for help, who, if they found no one in at the manse, would break in and help themselves. It might be tourists, visitors or schoolchildren learning about this lovely medieval treasure on their doorstep with wonderful stories to tell. Or it might be young couples wanting to get married in this iconic and picturesque building that almost everyone felt they had a stake in. The congregation hardly got a look-in.

When I finally began to get my head around my context for ministry, I ended up writing about a theology of hospitality, in which the empty-handed stranger could turn out to be the bearer of priceless gifts and blessings. Christ comes to us in the stranger's guise. I always remember Church of Scotland minister Gilleasbuig Macmillan's little piece of advice to me when I started out in ministry: 'Be aware that every now and then it may well be your task to protect those on the fringe of the church from the people at the centre.' It was wise advice and my rediscovery of the value of a ministry of hospitality has been something I have carried with me to Greyfriars Kirk in Edinburgh, largely with the congregation's support.

Here on the Camino, I was learning what it means to be open and anticipate gifts even from the most unlikely people and circumstances. But that can only happen when you de-clutter and make space and open yourself to the idea, one that is deeply embedded in the biblical narrative, that it is the stone the builders reject, because it doesn't seem to fit, because it is odd-shaped and irregular, that turns out to be the most significant stone of all and holds up the entire structure. Settled institutions tend to find quirky and 'odd-shaped' people a source of irritation and threat, failing to recognise their value. We who inhabit church buildings ought to look up at the keystone of any arch in a church to be reminded of this.

The other lesson I was learning in the midst of all this empty-headedness was about the action of the Holy Spirit, as we religious people are wont to call her. The Bible is full of stories about prophets and visionary people, indeed Jesus himself, who enter into a drama, 'filled with the Holy Spirit', and end up creating a stir, usually after spending time in the desert or a holy place. This walk was teaching me that most of the time our minds are fairly cluttered.

They are filled not with the Holy Spirit but with our own daily thoughts, from shopping lists to anxieties, from mundane priorities to disabling feelings of guilt, not to mention all our plans, hopes and aspirations for the future and our prejudices about others. Our minds are full up most of the time with our own thoughts so there is very little room left over for anything to enter in from elsewhere. This emptiness on the Camino was turning out to be a gift, not something to worry about. Now, for perhaps the first time in my life, I had some space in which my mind might be filled with the Holy Spirit (or at least some kind of deeper and more reflective richness). The thoughts that were flitting through my mind and the experiences that I was having now were so much more interesting than the chaotic radio interference that is the usual state of my mind at home. At this point I remained confused but I knew that somehow, at the end of all this walking and space-making, some fresh thinking would surely emerge. I had no great aspirations to be a prophet in the wilderness, nor had I any particular need to effect radical change in my personal life, but I knew this interlude was coming at an opportune time, if only to re-energise me for what might happen next.

CHAPTER 11
Last Day in France

I have come across quite a few people in my time who have been deeply damaged by religion, made to feel ashamed or guilty or simply screwed up by it. I'll never forget an elderly lady who called at my house one day. Her husband had died that morning and she wanted to ask if I might conduct his funeral even though I had never known him and she had never come to the church. I agreed without hesitation, and the story that emerged over the next few days as we prepared for the funeral broke my heart. She was a profoundly spiritual person, but as a child growing up on the Isle of Skye, that Hebridean centre of music and Gaelic culture, her family had had a visit from the parish minister. She was about twelve years old and the minister saw her fiddle lying in the corner of the room. He told her this was the devil's instrument and that she would go to hell if she persisted in playing it. It was therefore not a surprise that she had not known how to go back to church or if she would have been welcomed. This minister succeeded both in ruining her musical career and distancing her from the Christian faith which she still felt drawn to but confused about. I cannot imagine the courage she had to summon to approach me on that day. I was honoured to be able to walk with her as she made arrangements to bury her husband.

The singer Donnie Munro, from the band Runrig, once told us when he came to preach a sermon at Greyfriars that there had been a number of evangelical revivals on the Isle of Skye in the nineteenth and twentieth centuries and members of his family had been caught up in the religious fervour. One of the boasts at the time of such 'movements of the Spirit' were about how many hundreds of fiddles, or 'devil's instruments', had been burned. Donnie said that one of the things that had motivated him in his musical career was to make the point that it ought to be possible to hold together a religious faith and a passion for the music and culture of one's place.

The poet Edwin Muir talked about the cold, heartless impact of the Calvinism that took such firm root in Scotland following the Reformation. He spoke of God as having been turned into 'three angry letters in a book', the mystery of the Divine 'bent into an ideological instrument' with which to intimidate people.

A friend of mine told me once that he heard a Highland Presbyterian minister preach on the story of the Prodigal Son and had announced to his congregation that, 'if that had been my son, I might have had him back, but I would not have had a party for him'. How we sometimes spectacularly miss the point!

Some of the most wonderful poets Scotland has ever produced have been deeply spiritual Gaelic speakers who have struggled to find room for their brand of spirituality within the dominant Calvinist religion of their context. Indeed, they have found the imposition of a sometimes hard and heartless religious ideology to be a major source of their inspiration, usually in the form of lament for the way in which people have been harshly judged and abused in the name of God for the good of their own soul.

As I headed towards Spain and the next section of my pilgrimage, I was consumed with a concern that religious faith is so prone to being hijacked and distorted that it is almost too dangerous for human beings to handle. The numbers through the centuries who have been damaged by religion are incalculable; people who hoped for kindness, acceptance or sanctuary have been met with stern judgement and bad grace.

Knowing I had only a month left to walk, I took a train to Saint-Jean-Pied-de-Port to restart my journey a little further on, so that I could hope to reach Santiago in the time I had given myself. The train journey took me past the town of Lourdes. As I looked from the train, I saw busloads of pilgrims undertaking a very different form of pilgrimage. It occurred to me that one of the challenges those of us in Scotland face in trying to revive an interest in pilgrimage is that if people know anything about it, they probably have this sort of thing in mind. A flight or coach trip to a holy place where people go in the hope of a miracle cure for some ailment. That has certainly been the tradition, even in Scotland, in the past. Robert the Bruce is supposed to have suffered from leprosy and made more than one pilgrimage to Whithorn in Galloway in the hope of finding a cure, but soon after his last trip there, in 1328, he died.

One of the saints whom I had noticed throughout my journey in France was St Roch. At first, I was puzzled by the regular depictions of him lifting his skirts and showing a mark on his leg. I had thought this to be a stigmata, though it seemed an odd place to have one. Then I read up about him and discovered that the reason he had become famous and one of the 'patrons' of the Camino is that he was supposed to have contracted bubonic plague and survived. The mark on his leg was all that was left of the illness, a scar which he enthusiastically showed off to anyone who asked as evidence of the miraculous power of pilgrimage. Though not associated with the Camino de Santiago – he came from Montpellier and travelled as a pilgrim to Rome – he has been adopted as a hero of the Camino community. Like St Francis of Assisi, he turned his back on earthly treasures and power and became a friend to the poor. It is my guess that this is why he was so enthusiastically embraced by the democratic spirit of the pilgrim.

I was becoming more and more convinced that the real miracle of the pilgrimage is not the healing cure to be found at a holy well or the pious vision gained amongst the bones of a saint. I certainly believe that both psychologically and spiritually a pilgrim journey can reconfigure our lives, but I am a total sceptic when it comes to the idea that arthritis or bubonic plague can be overcome by plunging into a well, however holy. The real miracle of the Camino is the journey itself. 'Home is the journey,' as many have said.

I began to wonder whether the word 'Camino' might be more useful than pilgrimage and that we should be cautious about using the word pilgrimage too much for fear of giving people the idea that you have to be deeply religious and believe in miracle cures before you can benefit from a journey like this. My experience so far had been that many of the people undertaking this walk had been doing it for vaguely spiritual reasons, but very few were actually engaged in an expressly religious or pious act. But even those who did not start out with particularly holy intentions were finding that the physical challenge of walking every day and the encounters along the way added up to a transformative and spiritual experience; dare I say it – a blessing?

Getting off the train in Bayonne, I was sure I could smell the Atlantic. I very swiftly found a hotel to stay in and made my way to bed.

CHAPTER 12

Into Spain

The day was grey and misty as the train made its way slowly up to Saint-Jean-Pied-de-Port, the last stop in France before the Chemin de St Jacques becomes the Camino de Santiago. It all looked quite Alpine, and it felt cold as we climbed into the Pyrenees. When the train arrived in Saint-Jean a good number of fellow pilgrims, along with their sticks, were disgorged from the train. I bought some food: more sausage, a baguette and some interesting-looking cheese in a resealable glass jar. I headed for the village. I went into a little pilgrimage centre in order to register myself as a pilgrim again and get my *créanciale* stamped. By this time it was mid-morning and the man behind the desk asked me how far I intended to walk today. I said I hoped to make it to Roncesvalles. He looked sceptical and said that was a fair distance to start at this late hour of the morning and that I should probably have set out much earlier. By my reckoning I could do this in about six or seven hours, so I politely ignored him and set off.

I wandered down through the village and arrived at a sort of citadel or hill fort. It was closed, and I was puzzled to know why there were no signs pointing pilgrims on their onward journey out of town as there appeared to be plenty of options. As I wandered about trying to give the impression that I knew what I was doing, but feeling both baffled and frustrated, I spotted some people who looked like pilgrims heading back into the village. Just as in Le Puy-en-Velay, I followed them nonchalantly, trying to give the impression that I knew exactly what I was doing. The irony wasn't lost on me that at a second major starting point I had headed off at a fair lick in entirely the wrong direction. Was the Camino trying to tell me something? How many times had I done just that sort of thing in daily life? In a fit of excitement and anticipation it is so easy to allow a rush of blood to the head to take us off course. My instinct that Spain 'must be that way' was wrong by 180 degrees. I headed back up the main street and passed the pilgrim centre for a second time, delaying my departure by a further half hour and then picked up the Camino.

There is a lovely arch that you walk through as you leave Saint-Jean on the track, marking the old city wall. In front is the river. I immediately remembered this place from the film *The Way*, which I had seen a few months before, in which Martin Sheen undertakes a pilgrimage walk. He does so in the place of his son, who, in the story, had headed out on his own pilgrimage journey and in the mountains above Saint-Jean had taken a wrong turning in the mist and walked off a cliff. In the light of my appalling sense of direction, I had better watch out.

The mist was beginning to lift and the day to warm up. The atmosphere of the Camino was noticeably different as I headed up towards Spain. At first I wasn't sure why this should be, but it didn't take long to realise that what made this part of the Camino different was that the pilgrims here were from every corner of the globe and that the predominant language on this part of the journey had changed from French to English. Another difference was the number of people. If I'd had my wits about me as I left the pilgrim centre in Saint-Jean I would have very quickly realised, as I headed off in the wrong direction, that you just have to follow the crowd. There were a lot more pilgrims. Indeed, it is reckoned that up to a quarter of a million people undertake this walk every year.

It is a steady climb out of Saint-Jean and the sun was now blazing down. I felt as fit as a fiddle. My time walking in France had been perfect by way of preparation; not only had I toughened up my feet, I had also got myself 'match fit', as it were, and I felt absolutely on top form. In addition, my bad ankle had completely healed, so I was ready for anything. According to the guidebook – I was now operating with John Brierley's excellent manual *A Pilgrim's Guide to the Camino de Santiago* – the total amount of climbing that day would be 1,390 metres, which is about 4,500 feet. As the sun beat down and I marched on and on, I found myself sweating copiously, but really enjoying the invigorating challenge of the hill climb. It is something I really love and, as long as you are not too worried about getting hot and bothered, it can be a marvellous workout. It is also reassuring that at the end of the day you can probably step into some clean evening wear, get your clothes washed, and look forward to freshly laundered gear the next day. I think I must have drunk a gallon of water that day but I don't remember having to stop for a pee once.

I passed numerous people and had the odd chat. As the day marched on, I marched on with it. Having reached the high tops of the Pyrenees the path began to level out a little. I thought it would be good to pause for some lunch. As I looked for a suitable place to stop, I happened to glance back down towards Saint-Jean and saw a remarkable sight. The whole valley had been enveloped in cloud, which was coming in my direction. Like a giant exhalation, it was creeping up the mountain. I sat down to eat a quick and quite delicious lunch. The bread tasted wonderful, the sausage just like it should taste and, as for the cheese, it was a magnificent accompaniment to it all. Just as I finished this epic lunch with a crunchy apple, the cloud caught up with me and I was enveloped in thick fog. The temperature dropped dramatically, as did the visibility, and I remembered the disaster that befell Martin Sheen's son in the film. It was a spur to move on and find the border, knowing that from then on I would start to go downhill and find myself out of the fog.

I walked on in the dim light and didn't stumble over a cliff but instead found a little single-track road and a man in a white van selling coffee and other goodies to passing pilgrims. On the side of his van he had written in felt pen a list of numerous countries, and against each country he was keeping count of the nationality of the pilgrims as they passed. There were many French and Italians, as might be expected; lots of Americans and Australians and a fair few Irish; lots of Germans and Dutch; and modest numbers of most other countries in Europe, as well as Koreans and a number of Latin Americans. There were, however, precious few from England and none from Scotland, until now. I got a whole new column to myself! I walked on highly chuffed. I also realised how much work we had to do to get people at home interested in pilgrimage once more.

At one time Scotland had been a pilgrimage destination to rival Santiago. The cathedral at St Andrews, now a ruin, was once a magnificent building that would have matched any cathedral in Europe for its scale. It was also the pre-eminent shrine of the Apostle Andrew and people flocked there just as they went to Santiago to remember James. The

Reformers decided that the veneration of relics was a form of idolatry. They also, with probably a degree of justification, saw how the whole pilgrimage industry laid itself open to fraud and manipulation.

There is a wonderful story of Johann Tetzel, the indulgence pedlar in Germany whom many identify as the one who ignited Luther's fire of indignation 500 years ago. Apparently, Tetzel was asked by a nobleman if a future sin could be forgiven. Tetzel immediately declared that this was certainly the case, but only if money were paid out straight away. Later the same nobleman surprised Tetzel on the road and gave him a beating, declaring that this was the sin that had already been forgiven!

There was also a trade in ancient relics that meant there were enough fragments of the True Cross to create a forest, let alone a single tree. Indeed, one of Scotland's treasures in the Middle Ages was the Holy Rood, a fragment of the True Cross that, along with the Scottish crown jewels, was an essential part of the ceremony of coronation. The ruins of the abbey that held the relics stand close to Scotland's new parliament and adjacent to the Palace of Holyroodhouse. The church, in medieval times, was wont to excommunicate powerful people at will, but given the right diplomacy and incentives they might be just as willing to cancel the excommunication. Robert the Bruce, King of Scots, was excommunicated at one time for the murder of John Comyn, a rival to the Scottish throne, but the Bishop of Glasgow, for reasons unknown, absolved him. Murder is murder, but if the wind blew in a certain direction and it suited the powerful people of the day then such misdemeanours could be overlooked.

I wonder what God thought about it all. The chances are he was never consulted. I found myself reflecting on the degree to which our certainties about God can be more of a reflection of ourselves and our agendas than anything to do with knowing the mind of God. It's a concept I find hard to live with. I have always tried to be very sparing in my use of that three-letter word, God, because it conjures up so many notions (and frequently negative ones) in people's minds, on the basis that they are being sold someone's very particular concept of what they mean by the word.

A friend, Justin, told me once that 'God made man in his own image and we've been trying to return the compliment ever since!' The need for humility is endless. William Elphinstone is often considered one of the greatest of Scotland's medieval bishops, having been Bishop of Aberdeen in the late fifteenth century, Lord Chancellor of Scotland and founder of Aberdeen University. He is reported to have said that 'those who live by the altar must also serve it'. Many have remarked that if there had been more people like him in charge of the Scottish church in the Middle Ages we might never have had a Reformation. Not only did the Reformers do away with pilgrimage after 1560, the fragment of the True Cross, the Holy Rood, was lost for ever, and the numerous wonderful buildings of medieval Christendom fell into ruin. In my view, in abolishing pilgrimage, the Reformers were targeting the wrong thing.

This journey was, I was becoming more and more sure, having a similar effect on me as it had on the medieval pilgrim. Pilgrims from all over Europe must have been meeting people from other places and exchanging their ideas and friendship. They must have been having those moments of enlightenment and reflection that I was having, and they must have been growing and thinking about their faith and what it all meant, free from the constraints and impositions of the institutional church. The taverns and refuges along the way may have been dens of iniquity where people could misbehave, as undoubtedly many did, but they were also schools of revolutionary thought and free expression, where pilgrims could share their insights and learn together without being dictated to by an authority figure who claimed to have all the answers.

I also feel sure that for many pilgrims, the significance of the destination diminished as they found the Spirit alive with them on the journey, in the heart of the stranger and the open hand of hospitality. If the Reformers wanted people to use their conscience, think for themselves and come up with their own, very personal, relationship with the universal mysteries – which is, I think, what they were trying to do when they argued against the divine right of kings and supported the idea of the priesthood of all believers – there is no better place to attempt this than on a pilgrimage, where all enjoy equal status. Whilst pilgrimage is making a comeback in Scotland, there are still people who are rooted in the tradition that suppressed it. They simply don't want to take a second look and reflect that this might have something to offer those who are searching for a deeper, more spiritual life.

A couple of miles on from the man with the van, I crossed the border into Navarre, and my hopes of dropping out of the cloud and into the sunshine were realised. The last half of the journey, mainly downhill to Roncesvalles, was done in glorious sunshine and warmth. It was a walk of about 32 kilometres with a good deal of it uphill, and I have to say that my feet were in wonderful condition – my ankle did not play up at all and I felt strong and fit.

On arrival in Roncesvalles, I was shepherded into the gigantic pilgrim hostel, a refugio, which has been run by the Augustinians since medieval times. A large, friendly man beckoned me towards the door, and there was no other option than to accept his hospitality. It was a vast building, recently refurbished, a complex place of efficient contemporary design imposed on medieval splendour. It all looked sleek and well run. There were rooms for boots and Camino sticks and a fancy kitchen for those who were self-catering. The washing facilities were impeccable, and I got all my gear washed and spun (a novel innovation that sadly was repeated nowhere else on the route) in double-quick time. The dormitory was huge and had individual, chest-height cubicles providing a modicum of privacy, but these did nothing to stop the sound of snoring from filling the room and echoing around the vaulted ceiling. The whole place, although operated by the Augustinian order, was manned entirely by volunteers. I did not see a single monk in the time I was there. The volunteers were mainly people of retirement age who had been on the Camino themselves in the past and had loved it so much they wanted to come back and be a part of it. They were filled with enthusiasm, wise advice and charm.

Once I had done all my ablutions I headed out to explore, find a beer and book my place at dinner. The form here, with so many pilgrims passing through, was a shift system. The first sitting for dinner was called and everyone with a pre-paid blue ticket was ushered into a vast dining room to have their pilgrim menu. Those of us with a pink ticket had to wait until the blue-ticket diners had had their fill and then we were summoned. It was all so slick. I have to say it was also a bit depressing. I didn't particularly want to be herded and bossed around as though I were at school. The food was the biggest let-down of the whole operation. This place was functioning on an industrial scale, processing vast numbers of pilgrims throughout the year. The pasta was limp and the sauce that went with it obviously came straight from a large catering tin. The piece of meat was of indeterminate origin and tough as shoe leather (or my old hat!) and the pudding was something I would have to get used to from now on as I progressed through Spain. It was what they called 'flan', and which, in the UK, we would call crème caramel. In spite of the rather dull food on offer, I wolfed it down. I guess with all that walking and sweating and hill-climbing in the course of the day I might even have eaten tripe. Well, perhaps not.

CHAPTER 13
A Pilgrim Community

At 6 a.m. prompt, the lights in the dormitory came on with a brightness and intensity that was impossible to sleep through, though some of our fellow pilgrims made a good effort (they had been switched off just as promptly at exactly 10 p.m. the night before). It was clear that the people at Roncesvalles wanted us out and on our way. As my fellow pilgrims began to stir it was quite a sight to see them all, in almost complete silence, undertake the solemn duty of packing their rucksacks, preparing their feet for the exertions of the day and generally bracing themselves for whatever would meet them on the trail. Dressed and fortified by a croissant-type pastry and a ghastly cup of coffee that I had extracted from a coin-operated machine in the kitchens, I headed out of the door in the dark to be met by the most horrendous downpour.

Once again I hesitated about the route to take, and the smiling man who had waved me in the night before very kindly grabbed my arm and pointed me in the right direction with a wink and a smile, just as I was about to head off back towards France. For the next three hours I walked without a stop in the emerging light. The downpour eased to a drizzle and then petered out. At about 10 a.m. I stopped at a van parked where the Camino crossed a quiet rural road next to what looked like a disused quarry. It was,

I have to confess, almost the first time I had looked up and taken in my surroundings. In the rain, I found it best to keep my head down and walk on. This place was hardly the prettiest introduction to Spain. But I sat down with my Kit Kat and some sugary liquid (that tasted completely foul, though my body told me it needed it) and thought I would try to be sociable. I was astonished that for the first time on my entire walk so far I was sitting next to a fellow Briton. His name was Terry and he came from Nottingham. He was one of those scarily fit retired people who had done a lot of hiking and climbing in his life in some quite remarkable places. He was an intrepid chap who had seized the first opportunity he had to retire early and make a full-time occupation of undertaking expeditions in every part of the world.

Before I knew it I had met another couple of fellow countrymen. Like buses, you never see them and then they come in a convoy. These were a father and daughter, he a television cameraman from Wales and his daughter, who was clearly keen to follow in her dad's footsteps, not as a pilgrim – she was hating the whole experience – but by doing a course at college that would enable her to enter the world of film-making. At this point, I wondered what it would feel like to tag along with a group for a while. I was intrigued to see that certain pilgrims were keen to team up and walk with others. Some, like me, tended to be lone wolves, content with their own company and pace. I thought I ought to be sociable. I also realised that this might be just the sort of thing that would make people's hearts sink. So I took a decision there and then that I would be friendly and chatty whenever the circumstance seemed right but I would not overstay my welcome and either push on alone or else stop and let others carry on. I also knew that I valued time to be alone with my own thoughts, parlous and vapid though they sometimes were.

Pressing on alone after a few minutes of chat I found myself in a thick woodland. I stopped to fiddle with my backpack and undertake some adjustments, and I listened to the conversations of pilgrims as they passed. It was interesting. Almost everyone now was speaking in English. As I sat and took in the scene, imagining myself as some medieval mendicant, I overheard an American approaching and announcing in a loud voice to his companion something along the lines of, 'I manage an investment portfolio of 50 billion dollars.' My heart groaned inwardly. I thought to myself, here is one to avoid. But it is so easy to rush to judge, and, as I discovered later on, Brian turned out to be a pleasant fellow with a fascinating story to tell.

I spent the night in a place called Larrasoana about 27 kilometres from Roncesvalles. If, after my experience the previous night, I had been worrying that all refugios in Spain would be equally slick and ordered, I needn't have. This place was a real contrast and run by a couple of hippy types who were incredibly laid-back. The dormitory we slept in had so many bunks that it was almost impossible to move around, and it looked like exactly the sort of place in which to be wary of picking up the odd bedbug. Thankfully, this didn't happen. The washing facilities were wretched and the bathrooms even worse, but somehow I managed to have a warm shower and felt much refreshed, ready to hit the town.

Larrasoana was a depressing conglomeration of scruffy buildings, pilgrim hostels and semi-industrial decay. The only place with any life was an indoor football stadium with a fibre-glass roof. There was continuous noise from there until about 10 p.m. All through the town there were slot machines, not for gambling but for buying food, which might have been something of a gamble too, as there were sandwiches for sale, and I couldn't help speculating just how long some of them might have been languishing in these strange glass boxes. Why can't they just have shops, I thought to myself? Eventually I found a place to eat, and I realised that I'd had almost nothing since my Kit Kat earlier in the day. I devoured another pilgrim menu, including flan. I could get used to this, I thought to myself, as I made my way back to the dorm, having also downed a fair ration of delicious Rioja.

In the dorm I settled onto my top bunk close to the window. The football match was still going strong in the now brightly illuminated building, and across the dorm a young Australian was being given some sage advice by another American, but not the same one I had seen earlier. I listened in, half-heartedly, and then quite intensely as the American started to give the young, impressionable Aussie a pep talk. It was clear that the American saw himself as a misfit and didn't much care for the rest of humanity. He was on the run from his family, his friends, and from any kind of commitment. That was all fine, but he was suggesting that this was the only authentic way to live your life.

I almost felt like interrupting and challenging him. It has always struck me that in many respects we are defined by our relationships, that no person is an island and that if we go off to 'find ourselves' we are more often than not 'found' by others rather than 'discovered' by ourselves. How can we develop at all if we are shut off from others? The desire to escape, to avoid all attachments, is sometimes borne of a fear of being hurt and an unwillingness to grow as a person and discover the things about ourselves that make us uncomfortable.

I felt that the American was making a virtue of being solitary, but I wondered if he was actually on the run from himself. He said that his entire life was in his rucksack. He also claimed to be rootless: had no address and refused to acknowledge any next of kin. All this, he said, aroused the suspicion of the authorities wherever he went. People are defined by their job, their home or their family and friends, so if you say you have none of these, others find it unsettling and get suspicious. He said he wanted nothing to do with any of the attachments most of us have and that he wanted to be judged simply for who he was. I reflected that just before I came on this journey, a friend of mine had told me that one of the friends she valued most was the person who consistently reminded her of what she was like and the effect she had on others. And of course, frequently, that's the last thing we learn about ourselves, which is why it's so valuable to have honest friends who are not afraid to tell us what we are really like.

In one respect, I thought he had a point, which was that on the Camino people are valued simply for being there. There is no hierarchy or status – you are just a pilgrim.

I don't know if the American was just flannelling, talking in this way for effect, but it was clear that he was making this young Australian think hard about his own life. He was, after all, on pilgrimage, and that was about reviewing one's life and embracing change. It felt as though this young chap was being proselytised by some kind of cult. I remember once meeting an old school-friend by chance on an Edinburgh street, years after we had left school. We recognised each other, but almost immediately I knew that there was something different about him. It turned out he had become a member of the Moonies. It was obvious he was no longer the same; something within him was being suppressed. I hoped that this young Australian had enough gumption not just to swallow all that he was hearing and be deluded into believing that this guy had found the answer to a contented existence. I felt that the American, for all his protestations to be travelling light and feeling good about himself, was quite a troubled man.

Attachments can be costly, of course; they can cause us pain and demand much of us, but we are defined by our attachments. I remember a wonderful reflection by C.S. Lewis, who suggested in *The Four Loves* that we must make ourselves vulnerable to others even if that means risking having our hearts broken.

> Love anything and your heart will be wrung and possibly broken. If you want to make sure of keeping it intact you must give it to no one, not even an animal. Wrap it carefully around with hobbies and little luxuries; avoid all entanglements. Lock it up safe in the casket or coffin of your selfishness. But in the casket, safe, dark, motionless, airless, it will change. It will not be broken; it will become unbreakable, impenetrable, irredeemable. To love is to be vulnerable.

I wondered for a while afterwards whether I should have spoken up, but it was a private conversation and I was content to think that life is full of all sorts of people and perspectives, and it would be interesting for this young Australian to make up his own mind. I suppose I was feeling a bit protective and wanted to save him from being seduced by a world view that ran counter to everything that I think makes us human. The playwright Dennis Potter coined the phrase, the 'ache of life': it's that which makes us feel alive as much as the joy.

The pilgrim way certainly provides many opportunities for just this kind of experience, as a community of searching, open souls growing in self-understanding through encounter with the strangers and companions on the journey.

CHAPTER 14

The Human Torch

The next day, I set off very loosely in the company of a small group led by Terry. My reason for doing this was that my head torch was in the bottom of my rucksack and it was pitch dark. Again, I cursed myself for being disorganised and a useless navigator, so I hovered in the background, keeping an eye on the lights in front of me. It always seemed that everyone else was far more chummy and intimate with each other than I was with any of them, and far more organised.

As the light began to invade the path, we came upon a magical little place. At a small hamlet, the pangs of hunger having kicked in after a few miles of walking on an empty stomach, there was a little house, the courtyard of which had been turned into a small café. A group of young men, all looking rather cool, and clearly Camino veterans themselves, were preparing all sorts of breakfast delights, from freshly prepared tortilla to waffles, delicious sandwiches and a variety of cold meats. It was a welcome break and a delightful little moment of sociability and good humour.

Something else I was beginning to notice on the Spanish part of the Camino was a wonderful sense that the communities through which it wends its way offer huge amounts of support as well as respect for pilgrims. The cynic might say that this river of humanity provides an economic opportunity for those who live along the route. These young men had certainly found a source of income that would be especially welcome in these hard-pressed economic times in Spain. However, there has been a long association going back a thousand years, a symbiotic relationship, between residents and those passing through. There was a genuine friendliness on the part of many of the people I passed. I have no doubt that many of those who lived along the route had done the walk at some time in their lives and knew something of its transformative power. You might imagine that this steady stream of humanity might be a bit tiresome for the locals, but it wasn't that way at all. Again, I kept thinking back to the insight that you bring your welcome with you, inasmuch as if you go around with a grumpy hostile look on your face you are more than likely to get that back, but if you look ready to smile and feel at peace with the world and yourself, you'll get good things in return.

As I approached the city of Pamplona it became obvious that we were in the Basque country. There were slogans everywhere, graffiti on every bridge and wall and even on the pavements. Much of it was in English and presumably for the attention of pilgrims, mainly informing us that the struggle for independence and self-determination was not over, even though the violence and bombing had now more or less ceased. It was interesting to read that one of the most dangerous parts of the Camino for the medieval pilgrim was the Basque country, as the region was notorious for its bandits. That is probably the reason why Pamplona has the most enormous Knights Templar castle at its heart – they must have been busy protecting pilgrims in this region. Pamplona is a big city of about 200,000 people. Its bull-running was made famous by Ernest Hemmingway in his novel *The Sun Also Rises*.

I'd had a conversation about bull-running with someone who had suggested that it is something you need to do at least once in your life. I am not sure I understood why he said that. Is it something to do with proving manliness, or having a brush with death? It is also an opportunity for the local people to let their hair down and have a *festa*. The festival of San Fermín is a bizarre tradition in which men – and I think it remains exclusively a male activity – risk their lives by running ahead of six bulls on a course down one of Pamplona's narrow cobbled streets. The course finishes at the bullring, where a bullfight takes place later in the day at which all the bulls are dispatched. This happens every day for a week at the beginning of July and is a tradition that goes back to at least the thirteenth century. It is associated with the legend of St Fermín, a third-century convert to Christianity and one of the patron saints of Navarre who may have lost his life after being dragged through the streets by a bull.

The walk through the city must have been about ten kilometres with a pause at the cathedral, Santa María la Real. It costs €7 to get in but if you have a pilgrim passport you can enter for €3 and you get a nice badge. This was the first major church I had visited since arriving in Spain. I had popped into many French churches along the Chemin de St Jacques and they were invariably open. It was almost always possible to spend a little time, light a candle and reflect. I had read that in Spain the churches were frequently closed.

The first thing to strike me when I wandered into the cathedral was the gold. There was gold everywhere. The Spanish conquest of South America had brought back vast quantities of the stuff, even if the major hoard of gold from El Dorado remains hidden. It was a level of ornateness and opulence that my Presbyterian stomach found hard to cope with, and I couldn't help but reflect on the butchery and plunder that characterised the colonisation of the Americas by the Conquistadores. I also couldn't forget all those true heroes of pilgrimage, like St Roch, Santo Domingo and St Francis, who'd taken vows of poverty and simplicity of life in order to pursue a faithful journey of solidarity with the poor and the vulnerable. Such a contrast to the ostentatious show of this vast cathedral. It was a shrine to wealth, power and plunder, and Jesus himself would have felt quite uncomfortable in it.

As I wandered around, a small army of ladies were mopping and polishing around the altars and shrines and the place didn't lend itself to any kind of spirituality. I think that what killed it for me and summed the place up was that there were no candles to light. Instead, you had to drop a coin in a slot and a little candle-shaped electric light would come on, giving you, I should imagine, a fifteen-minute connection to the Almighty until the money ran out and you had to dig around for another euro. It felt like indulgences all over again. I decided not to stay for too long in the cathedral, but after finding a rather splendid ancient loo in the cloister, I discovered that the heavens had opened and there was a downpour outside. So I changed my mind and decided to get interested.

I slipped back in and tried my best to give the appearance of being genuinely curious to learn about the history of the cathedral and give the impression of piety. One of the highlights is the burial place of Carlos el Noble, King of Navarre. He was responsible for completing the cathedral, and you cannot help but think that this place is more a shrine to him and his wife Eleanor, who lie side by side in the heart of the building, than it is a place of worship.

In spite of this, Charles the Noble does seem to have been quite a good egg in comparison to his father, Charles the Bad. Charles the Noble was at heart a peacemaker, seeking to create a stable country and live well with his neighbours. His father, by contrast, was an out-and-out rogue and schemer, changing sides in wars at regular intervals, organising murders and, in his jealous rage, mounting land-grabs to build up his influence and power. Charles the Bad's death has to be one of the most horrific on record. He was apparently extremely stiff and had little use of his limbs, and his doctors advised that he should be wrapped in linen sheets soaked in brandy. In this mummified state, his doctors then ordered that he be sewn in to keep the linen nice and tight. One of his attendants, who was busy stitching the poor king up, had difficulty cutting a piece of thread and went for a candle to burn through it. Then – whoomph! The king died as a human torch – horrendous!

After my little bit of research, I checked outside and saw that the rain had stopped, so I continued my march through the streets of Pamplona and found my way to Cizur Menor, a pleasant and fairly affluent suburb where the girls at the local school all wear tartan skirts. The albergue had a beautiful garden with a large and ferocious-looking dog on a chain. The sun shone but the air was very chilly and I almost didn't have enough clothes to wear. As I went about the afternoon ritual of claiming my bed (near a window and a door and as far away from potential snorers as possible), unpacking my gear, and washing myself and my kit, various people I had met over the last day or so began to arrive. There was Terry from Nottingham; Myron, who ran a coffee house in the American Midwest; and Brian, whom I had heard talking loudly about how much money he managed.

The four of us were joined by a young Danish woman called Katrine. We sat around chatting, laughing and teasing each other until it was time to saunter off into town and find a place to eat. It was a very convivial evening, and I was really impressed by Katrine, who was able to stand up to four men in their fifties who all had her best interests at heart and probably sounded like a group of dads. She was full of fun, gave as good as she got and really tapped into the humour of a bunch of dry-witted old men who were full of nonsense. It is always refreshing to come across people who don't take themselves too seriously, and my new male chums were certainly in that category.

At the restaurant, the pilgrims were all shunted off into a dining room and given the traditional menu. Again it felt a bit like being at school. The food was always basic, with the ubiquitous flan to finish off, but I liked the menu choice of water or wine at the same price. Invariably people had both.

In the bar after dinner we chatted some more, and then the thing I dreaded came up. We had to own up to what we did in our non-Camino life, and so it came out that I was a minister. My reluctance to divulge the truth harked back to Grégoire's comment that when he was on the Camino he forgot his other life, but it was also borne of the consistent experience of finding that people end up making all sorts of assumptions about you. They assume you must be devout, and I have often confounded people by admitting that I am frequently confused, doubting and reluctant. I have never felt terribly 'religious', but I am an ardent fan of Jesus and more interested in the mystical than the ecclesiastical. I learned a long time ago that I am certainly not the person with the most unshakeable faith in my congregation, and I have often felt that my call to ministry came about as part of a search to explore with others the great mysteries, not in order always to give answers to deep questions, but to enable a journey, a pilgrimage if you like, more deeply into the unfathomable nature of existence. I also became a minister for very similar reasons that had led me to study law many years ago. I wanted to work for social justice and to enable the voices of those who inhabit the margins of society to have their wisdom, insight and experience heard. Whilst I have always felt a deep loyalty to Jesus of Nazareth, as 'the Son of Man', I constantly wrestle with religious ideas, the institutions of the church and the idea that faith demands the suspension of reason and intelligence and the embrace of dogmatic principles. I think of faith as a very practical thing, a relationship of trust, if you like, rather than a series of propositions. If I were to say I believe in Martin Luther King, it wouldn't be saying much about him if it were merely my opinion that he had existed. To believe in something, someone, or in a movement like the human rights campaign Martin Luther King spearheaded, or to express a belief in God, is a very practical act of putting your trust in something, not expressing an opinion that they exist or don't.

One of the other reasons for being reluctant about owning up to what I do, and this must be a problem that many others face, is that people can start to share with you their inmost feelings and woes, and before you know it you are in the midst of a pastoral encounter. That is fine, except that sometimes it is good just to have a bit of time for oneself, and this Camino experience was my time. Anyway, they got it out of me, and no one seemed to be too surprised. Meanwhile, it turned out that Brian was indeed a fund manager back in California, Myron ran his coffee shop, Terry had been an engineer and Katrine was about to embark on law studies in the next year or so.

I can't think why I remembered this at that moment, but an episode about people's jobs came back to my mind very vividly from many years previously. I had arranged to meet up with some pals to do some hillwalking in the Knoydart peninsula in the north-west of Scotland. We gathered in Mallaig on the Sunday evening, having made arrangements to be taken over to Knoydart by boat the following day. After pitching our tents just outside the village in the early evening, we made our way to the pub for some seafood and beer. As the evening wore on an inebriated regular staggered over to us to engage in conversation, always a moment to test the powers of tolerance. After a while he began to ask what jobs each of us did. Marcus volunteered that he was an accountant, Chris, a lawyer, Neil a graphic designer and Angus a doctor, but before I got the chance to say what I did for a living, the man pointed at me and blurted out, 'And I bet this guy's a f****** minister!'

This little group proved to be a lot of fun. Myron and I had shared the dormitory with Brian the previous night and, as I had said to him, Brian was only great company as long as he was awake. In his sleep, he had a staggering capacity for an ear-splitting snore. The other presence in this dormitory was the intense American who had regaled the young Australian the previous night with his philosophy of life. Once again he slipped silently out before anyone else was awake and was on the trail by 5 a.m.

CHAPTER 15

The Pilgrim's Tale

Leaving Cizur Menor, the trail took me over stubble fields and a slight incline towards the hills. The sun rose and all the world turned a golden harvest colour. It was cold in the early morning but it promised to get warmer as the day wore on. It was a steady trudge uphill most of the morning, and I passed a young woman who asked me if I had some spare water. She had forgotten to fill her flask up at the start of the day and needed some refreshment as the day began to warm up. I gave her a bottle of water and we walked on together for a short while. Carolein was from the Netherlands. She worked with young people with behavioural problems back home and had seen the Camino as a chance to recharge her batteries and get fresh energy for what was a very trying job. I wished her well and then, once we reached a village where she could resupply herself with water, I bade her farewell and pressed on.

By now the terrain was steeper; I had entered an area of scrubland. Above was a massive line of wind turbines stretching for miles along a ridge. I began to understand why the Spanish were so involved in renewable energy technologies in Scotland. At the top of the ridge Alto del Perdon, or the Hill of Forgiveness, the view across the plains that stretched ahead towards La Rioja and Logroño made Spain feel immense and rather daunting. At the top of the ridge there is a cast-iron sculpture of a group of pilgrims bending themselves against the wind to make their way onwards. It was certainly a well-chosen site for a wind farm, and it was possible to see the evidence of just how committed they are in Spain to this form of energy production. There were turbines all over the place as far as the eye could see.

The rocky descent from the ridge led to Puente la Reina with its magnificent six-arched Romanesque bridge built in the eleventh century to carry pilgrims safely on their way across the River Arga and doing a valiant job still in the twenty-first. According to the guidebook, this was the place to stop. I paused just over the bridge to chat with Katrine, who was fiddling with her boots – both of us had decided to walk much further today. It also occurred to me, seeing that so many people had a copy of John Brierley's guide to the Camino in their packs, that most people were following his instructions to the letter. The last thing I wanted to do was to be a sheep doing what I was told the whole time, so I decided that I would branch out, be radical, walk a little further and stay somewhere that only gets a passing mention in the guide.

Katrine and I walked on together for a short while, and then we parted company as she nursed some emerging blisters. I wondered if I should hang around and offer to assist her, but she was a plucky sort and was quite determined to deal with her problems on her own. It was getting quite hot and there were more hills to climb. I pressed on, arriving at a small village called Cirauqui in the late afternoon. I had decided that every now and then I would treat myself to a decent hotel room, and the experience of the pilgrim hostels had confirmed that this was a good move. The nightly decibel level was unremitting, and it seemed only reasonable every now and then to find a single room and have a peaceful night's sleep. I should have known better.

I found a delightful, simple and cheap hotel just opposite the church in Cirauqui. Outside the town hall were two large effigies of a king and queen, at least 15 feet tall. As I settled into my little room, I washed my clothes in the sink and hung them out over a balcony with the most stunning view out of the village and across the plain ahead. The road I would follow the next day was down below (it was always reassuring to have a glimpse of where I might be heading in the morning as invariably it would still be dark when I set off – a great opportunity to get fantastically lost). This road out fascinated me as it was described as one of the best-preserved Roman roads in the whole of Spain. The sun was flooding into my room and my clothes, out on the line, were dry in no time.

Outside, I made my way into the square. Things were hotting up. The effigies of the king and queen had made their way from the lower square and were now loitering outside the church whilst what seemed like the entire village was in the church singing some lusty Basque carol. A mixture, I surmised, of piety with patriotism, always very dangerous. But it made me think about the powerful sense of identity that people still share in Spain. Language, culture and tradition are deeply important, and the stories being re-enacted here demonstrated a tangible sense that this community was bound together by a shared narrative that was still exerting a powerful influence in spite of all the drivers of modernity.

As the villagers came out of the church, nearly all of them were wearing red neckerchiefs. In deference to the spirit of the party I whipped out a bandana from my pocket and tied it round my neck. The crowd proceeded from the church to the square a little further down, where a large stage had been erected and the festivities began in earnest. I met Myron, and we bumped into a young man called Will who had just graduated from university and was taking some time to decide what to do with the rest of his life and thought the Camino would provide a good place to think. We have stayed in touch and I know that Will seems to have found the thing he went walking to discover: he is making a career out of being a professional walker. As I write this I think of that man I met back in France at Le Domaine du Sauvage who suggested that some people get the pilgrimage bug and just have to keep on walking for the rest of their lives.

Carolein and another Dutch woman were staying in the village, and soon the party was in full swing. More and more people poured into the square. The king and queen began to bop around to the music and people welcomed the strangers in their midst with tolerance and grace. They were so used to this stream of humanity from every corner of the globe that we felt accepted. I suppose in any other village not on the Camino a selection of foreign visitors sharing in a village party would have created a bit of a stir, but here strangers passing through were part of the furniture.

The party went on and on, and soon my Camino friends sloped off to their beds, weary after the day's exertions. I too didn't last long and headed for bed. My hopes of a quiet night's sleep were thwarted, however, when I realised that the party only reached its zenith at around 3 a.m. with an almighty firework display. After that, I thought I was just dreaming that the party carried on, but it wasn't a dream. When I left my little hotel at about 6.45 there were still crowds of now thoroughly inebriated partygoers crawling around the square. The mess and the stench of spilled alcohol was horrendous. I made my way to the Roman road, reflecting that Spain may be in the midst of a huge recession but they still know how to party.

That Roman road was a remarkable start to the day. It was in pristine condition. It felt as though the scene I was walking through had changed very little for centuries, and I began to reflect that people actually change very little too. It is only the clothes and the walking kit that are different; the life of the inner self is the same. This notion of being lost in time was rapidly becoming a major feature of my Camino experience. The gap between the life we lead today and that of people, even a generation or two ago, seems to be yawning and huge. But here amongst these ancient buildings, along a route that had been laid down by Romans who saw the potential of the north of Spain as a grain basket to feed the empire and which had been marched along by pilgrims for a thousand years, all that separated me from those ancient times seemed to be of little consequence. The combination of walking and the landscape evoked feelings that could not be so different to the moods and feelings of those who had walked this way before me. It felt that this was an important point that the Camino was making to me. In its gentle way, it was reminding me that human beings are much the same, regardless of the age in which we live.

I arrived in Estella in the late morning and met up once again with Myron. I shared with him my intention to take a detour through a more rugged and rural route on the last part of the day's journey to Los Arcos. Myron wondered if I would like company to do this detour over the hills and through the woods, and we agreed to spend the rest of the day walking together. The route took us uphill and into a beautiful pine wood. It was the first sustained period of walking and talking with another person that I had done since Jon had left me back in France many days before.

The hours that followed proved to be an affirmation of the power of the pilgrimage to promote unexpected and enriching communication, to inspire spontaneous friendship and to enable a healing exchange to take place. But before we took our detour we had another rather delightful experience to share together.

Just beyond Estella I had seen on the map a tantalising sign: 'fuente del vino'. The pilgrim community had shared the rumour of this magical place – a wine fountain! We didn't wait long to find out what this could be. Just a few kilometres out of Estella we saw looming up before us a huge wine factory, the Bodegas Irache. The path passes this large industrial building, and built into the wall in a shaded area are two taps. One tap dispenses water and the other, fine Rioja wine. A free gift from the bodega to the pilgrim community. Well, it is not hard to think what you are supposed to do. As someone once said to me, 'If a horse falls out of the sky, you don't examine its teeth'. My only regret was that I didn't have more containers, but I emptied what I had and filled up with wine. It was becoming a warm day and as tempting as it was to fill all my water containers with wine, I knew that this would be a crazy thing to do. The thought of becoming dehydrated and having only wine to drink in that heat was not pleasant.

Just after the fuente del vino we left the main path, set off uphill and realised that it was indeed going to be a hot afternoon. The cloudless sky, the brown, parched earth and the smell of the sap from the pine trees gave a real sense of being out in nature, and this was only enhanced by the fact that there were now very few people on this trail that was going to add an extra 12 kilometres to our day's route. As we ascended steadily, I was aware of that horrible tendency I have already alluded to of wanting to extend myself on steep inclines. Myron kept up, but his first confession was the fact that over the last year he had shed an enormous amount of weight. He said that before coming on the Camino he had been doing a huge amount of cycling and had lost as much as 50 pounds in a regime designed to regain fitness. It had clearly worked. Although he was two or three inches shorter than me, he was quite lean and fit and was certainly no heavier than I was. The combination of the heat and the punishing uphill section was not posing him too many worries. He said that a year ago this walk would have destroyed him. It was wonderful to meet someone who had taken such control of his life and his health, and was working his way back to fitness. It was, in fact, quite hard to imagine him as the overweight person he described.

The conversation naturally led to the circumstances in which he had put on the weight in the first place. That was when the second confession was made. Myron admitted that the other night he had not been entirely straight with our fellow walkers when we had admitted to what our work was. Certainly he ran a coffee house, but he was also an ordained minister. Somehow this news did not entirely surprise me. I don't know what it is, but occasionally you can just tell. I have often wondered if it is something like the idea of the 'shaman' – a person, usually in a tribal or traditional community, who acts as an intermediary between the visible world and the invisible, spirit world.

I suppose within Christianity there are those who consider that faith is something that is revealed or mediated through scriptures and through the church and its doctrine.

There are others of us who also believe that the Spirit of God is at loose in the world and is not confined to ecclesiastical structures, and that the untamed wildness of the Divine can be caught by people who have very little to do with organised religion.

Every now and then, though not very often in 'King Calvin's Kirk', you meet a fellow minister with that inner eye, that shamanic quality that has drawn them to the vocation of being the one with the spiritual antennae switched on for the sake of the community. My sense about Myron was that he was one of those who carried that mark about him. It was possible to discern a kind of spirituality in the manner in which he carried himself, a sort of light in the eye. I am not saying that such a condition carries any special virtue or merit, it is just a consequence of how some people are made. But how did being a minister make him put on so much weight? Well, that is the story he unfolded to me as we walked together along the way.

He had grown up in a strict Brethren community, but over the years had found this straightjacketed approach to religion less and less appealing. Gradually he had migrated into a more mainstream, but still evangelical, church and had become involved in college chaplaincy work. Then he revealed to me, in a sort of confession, I suppose, something that to my liberal mind simply beggared belief. His congregation had discovered that in the 2008 presidential election he'd voted for Barack Obama. My first reaction was to say, 'So what?' But he went on to say that when they had discovered how he had voted they began an enquiry. They disciplined him, hounded him and persecuted him. 'For voting Democrat?' I exclaimed, still not quite able to grasp why this should have upset people as much as it did.

'Well, don't you know that a lot of Americans think Obama is a communist, while others think he is an Islamist extremist? And of course, he is pro-choice.' Myron explained further, 'How could a minister of religion vote for a man who was in league with the devil?'

It seemed extraordinary to me that such an inquisition should take place in a country that cherishes freedom of speech and liberty of conscience. The persecution and questioning and negative judging went on for months, and the poor man was deprived of his living, his house and his ministry. That is how he ended up running a coffee shop. His faith had been rocked, but he remained committed to a vocation of hospitality, a ministry of welcome that acknowledged the inner life of the Spirit expressed in creating a nurturing and welcoming community. But now he was doing it through a coffee house, not a church.

What a post-modern story, and what an indictment of the way in which organised religion can sometimes turn into a tyranny, especially when those who wield authority believe that they have the last word and all the answers, and everyone else is misguided. I am coming more and more to believe that the institutions of religion are only capable of being healthy when we really understand at a deep level their provisional nature. Surely, it must be obvious that none can have complete knowledge and understanding of the mystery of the Divine, yet we have rarely built flexibility, humility and openness to new insight into them. Maybe we need more coffee-shop churches.

As we walked, I thought of these two disciples on the road to Emmaus (perhaps a husband and wife, as only one of the two, the man, gets a namecheck, which is telling in itself), out on their own pilgrimage, trying to get their heads around all that had happened in Jerusalem to their leader, Jesus of Nazareth. And how, as they walked, they remembered the way in which Jesus had been hounded and persecuted and put to death by the ecclesiastical authorities, the very people who ought to have known how to catch that wind of God that blows where it wills. The authorities found this man troublesome and a threat and so had him arrested on jumped-up charges and eventually hung up to die on a cross. What Myron had just shared with me was a similar story to the experience Jesus had: the hounding and persecution of an innocent man by ecclesiastical authorities.

Inwardly, I wept for this good and kind-hearted man. All the misery and false accusations and even the ecclesiastical courts that his congregation set up to hear him and condemn him had not led to an execution on the hill of Golgotha, but it had almost broken him. He had resorted to overeating; it had taken its toll on his family. But in the last year he had battled back. He had undergone his own resurrection and had cast off the weight that he had put on. The crowning moment was this pilgrimage, this journey back to life. I felt for him and all he'd gone through, but I was also filled with gratitude that he had chosen to share his story with me.

For many people the pilgrimage journey starts from a position of belief, a desire to nourish one's spiritual life, but to do so in the expectation of discovering riches as yet unknown by undertaking the rigours of the journey, away from the familiar and the secure and with an open heart. In the encounter with the stranger on the pilgrim way, there is a willingness to create that open space in which fresh perspectives and new insights might be gained, and, just possibly, the risen Christ might be encountered in the stranger's guise. This is not to devalue or erode one's own faith or to embrace an alternative for its own sake. Rather, the pilgrimage turns out to be an experience in which faith is deepened and enriched. An authentic pilgrim is willing to be 'stretched' both physically and spiritually by journeying to that space in which we can learn from 'the committed nature of others' whose spiritual journey can inform and deepen our own.

That, to me, is what pilgrimage is all about, and I had learned that in such a huge way by hearing Myron's story and walking with him. It felt such a privilege. It may be that the starting point of a pilgrimage emerges out of some ecclesiastical duty, but ultimately the point of the thing is the formation that takes place in the mind of the pilgrim. The holy destination, the ecclesiastical authority, is almost completely irrelevant.

One of my theological heroes is Donald Mackinnon. He was Professor of Divinity at Cambridge University but retired back to Aberdeen where he had previously been Professor of Moral Philosophy. I got to know him briefly as a very old man just before he died in 1994. Mackinnon was a Scottish Episcopalian who had been launched into the world of Anglo-Catholicism, first at Oxford in the 1940s and 1950s and then at Cambridge. He had spent much of his life asking the question, 'How can the church represent the manner of God's presence to the world in Christ?' His conclusion increasingly led him to see that as a power structure the church had adopted the clothes of empire ever since Constantine the Great made Christianity the official religion of Rome. The Pope was in a sense an absolute monarch, and the manner of Jesus's activity in Galilee had been almost entirely obscured by the power structures that had developed down the centuries. Mackinnon came to see that Christ had divested himself of almost all forms of temporal power. He may have had a huge amount of spiritual strength, but he wielded no political power whatsoever. If the church was to 'be the Christ' to others, it would have to have the courage to do something similar and shake off its desire for power.

Of course, people may say that even Jesus used the language of kingship, but he was not speaking of a political kingdom. He describes the kingdom with a succession of stories, metaphors and parables that subvert models of political power. It is as if the kingdom he had in mind was so far beyond the reach of the imagination of people, so alternative, that he had to illustrate it with pictures: the kingdom is like buried treasure, a pearl of great price which a merchant bought by selling all he had to attain it; it is like a great feast to which everyone is invited but no one turns up; it's an unlikely, tiny seed that turns into a noble tree giving shade to those who sit under it.

For many hundreds of years, and even into the present, Christ's church has been a hugely influential power structure. And the Christian empire has been substituted for the Kingdom of God. For all that it has produced its fair share of saints and heroes, it has also produced a fair number of phoneys and crooks. The Anglican liturgical scholar Gregory Dix once remarked that it was no accident that the emblem of a bishop should be a crook and that of an archbishop a double cross! (But there are plenty of phoneys in every branch of the church, I am not just singling out bishops!) The point is that the Christian empire has often been more of a 'ground for boasting than it has been an opportunity for presence', as Donald Mackinnon put it.

As we walked along in the blistering afternoon heat, I began to feel a sense of the subversive power of the Camino. Mackinnon had guessed that the Galilean peasant Jesus of

Nazareth had inaugurated a movement that had been hijacked and at times had lost its way. On the pilgrim trail, hearing each other's stories, connecting and making friendship, we found Christ walking with us, illuminating a way into a new kind of community in which each one matters, regardless of status and story. Good and bad alike, sinner and holy, all were one on the Camino, and the magic of it was in the human exchange and the creation of a community of mutual respect, belonging and trust, devoid of hierarchy. Jesus put humility and mercy in the place of power and authority, and that's what I found on the road.

We came out of the forest and descended down onto the plain as the heat began to rise and the sun blazed on our backs. It felt good to be out and to be making headway. Myron and I had found a kind of instant friendship on the Camino. We had established a relationship of trust, mutual respect and openness that, in other circumstances, might have taken years to achieve.

We came into the tiny village of Luquín and were able to get some water at a huge stone trough by the roadside. As we filled our water bottles and gulped down great globs of water, a passing farmer shouted at us from his tractor cab. Initially, it was all quite disconcerting. Why was this man being so rude to a couple of innocent passing pilgrims? Only after a few moments of wild gesticulating and looks of crestfallen reproach from us did we notice that all the while he was pointing towards a sign above the trough that declared the water to be undrinkable and dangerous. Instantly, my heart sank. I could feel my guts starting to churn. I was convinced that I would be convulsed with nausea that would lead to a rapid decline into a painful, agonising dose of poisoning, or worse.

I managed to pull myself together as we spotted a little swimming club not far ahead. We wandered into the bar there and found some drinkable water and a sandwich to keep us going for the next stage to Los Arcos.

As we rejoined the main path we found ourselves in almost desert-like terrain. The sun beat down, the vegetation was very sparse and there were no houses or settlements of any kind. There were also very few people. We guessed that most of the people walking this way today would already have passed by, as their destination would be Los Arcos, which they would anticipate reaching in the late afternoon. I found myself feeling exhilarated to be in an area that was so remote, with few people around. I could sense Myron being a little anxious – the heat was clearly getting to him now – but I'd like to think he felt somewhat reassured to be in company. By now the water that we had taken on board had long since been sweated out and the bottle I had with me had only about an inch of liquid left in it. It was now tepid and tasted quite foul. But the refreshment it brought with each tiny sip was pure nectar, and I was reminded just what a delicious and perfect drink water is. Anything else in this heat would have been utterly unsatisfactory.

After about five kilometres we noticed a small group of people up ahead. They were sitting together under the only tree for miles around. As we came closer we could see that below the tree was a dried-up riverbed. One of the people in this little group was an Italian I had seen the previous day. He was walking with a large dog that had thick, dark curly hair. It was clear that the dog was in some distress and looked barely able to stand in the heat; the poor thing must have been terribly dehydrated. There was really nothing that anyone could do but exchange a few encouraging words and trust that everyone would find enough energy to carry on and get to Los Arcos and a source of water.

We pressed on, and as we moved over some low hills I kept saying to Myron that over the next rise we'd be bound to catch our first glimpse of Los Arcos. No such luck. All we saw was miles and miles of this barren and unforgiving landscape. No sign of human habitation, just a snake of the pilgrim path leading to the next rise. On we slogged. Secretly, I felt on top of the world. This was walking with a real challenge, some sense that what was required was a bit of steely resolve and determination. I remained nauseatingly cheerful and optimistic, but thankfully Myron proved to be a tolerant and kindly companion, and he put up with my breezy manner. Thankfully also, there were absolutely no signs of imminent nausea or death from our unfortunate drinking bout at the stone trough back up the road.

After another hour or so we spotted a lone figure on the path up ahead. At first, it seemed like the figure was a good mile away, so I subconsciously doubted that, even at our fair speed, we would be able to overtake them (that hideous streak of competitiveness coming out yet again)! However, as we walked on the figure loomed rapidly closer. Clearly he or she was moving very slowly. I began to wonder if my mind was playing tricks and that in the heat and the intense sunshine the person had looked much further away than was the reality. Only when we came closer did we realise that the woman, as she turned out to be, was on her feet but barely moving forward. By my very rough calculation we were still about six kilometres from Los Arcos and it was now about five in the afternoon. That meant we'd get there in about two hours, but this lady would be lucky to be there by midnight at the pace she was going.

We came alongside and began to speak. She was French and had no English. She explained that she was suffering from terrible blisters and was exhausted too. She said that she had plenty of water and was absolutely determined to walk on, on her own and at her own pace. She did not want any help and was adamant that she would be fine. She also indicated that this was all part of the pilgrimage and that she was sure she would not die out on the trail.

We were not so sure. But we were not about to try to overrule her, and anyway, I might have got my calculations wrong; it was possible that Los Arcos was indeed just over the next horizon. After a few more exchanges of broken conversation and offers of help, we abandoned the poor woman to her fate. At least, we thought, there were no bandits or wolves to tear her to shreds. But after a few minutes Myron admitted that he felt uneasy. We had after all just walked away from someone who was in no fit state to cover more than a few hundred yards in an hour. We decided that as soon as we arrived in Los Arcos we would report that there was an ailing pilgrim some miles back up the trail. Surely this sort of thing happened the whole time; people wouldn't be left out to die?

In another hour or so we saw the first buildings we'd seen for many miles – the outskirts of Los Arcos. And what a sight of desolation they proved to be. You couldn't have contrived a scene from some western better. A few ramshackle buildings in various states of disrepair clung on to the edge of the desert. You'd expect to see Clint Eastwood's horse tied up to a post and a few grim-looking honchos lurking furtively in the shade under wide-brimmed sombreros.

We reached the first building in the town, and inside a great cavernous barn there was a slot machine dispensing various liquids, including, thank God, water. I had some coins in my pocket and purchased three bottles, which I consumed instantly. All of this we did while being observed from the same building by a geriatric lady from an upstairs window. She never smiled, returned my salutation or showed any sign of being alive – she just stared at us. After finishing the water we moved on, waving to the motionless lady as we went. I was now convinced she was a stuffed dummy. We headed for town. It was still another mile or so until we came across the familiar sight of narrow cobbled streets, ancient buildings radiating from a central square and the obligatory gorgeous ornate basilica in the midst of it all, dedicated, naturally, to St James the Pilgrim.

For the first time on the entire Camino I received a rejection at a refugio. We wandered up to the entrance of the first hostel we could find and asked if they had a couple of beds left. I cannot remember the exact name the lady at the counter used but she said something like, 'Is your name Alberta Solari?'

To which I felt very tempted to reply, 'Do I look like an Alberta to you?'

She then went on to say that if my name was not Alberta then she had no beds, as someone called Alberta had called ahead and booked the last remaining bed and was expected any minute. We left the hostel feeling downcast and wondered if tonight might be the first night of sleeping rough. Just as we left we were greeted by the sight of the suffering French lady languishing in the back of a Land Rover. The vehicle pulled up and she smiled sweetly at us and muttered something that I took to mean, 'The spirit is willing but the flesh is weak,' and gave us a rather sheepish look. Then she was carried ceremoniously out of the Land

Rover and, like some ancient goddess, a small crew of strong men whisked her into the hostel. We never did learn her name, but of course it must have been Alberta. The sheepish look maybe had to do with the fact that she knew she had bagged the last bed in the place, pre-empting us by the use of her mobile phone, no doubt. Lucky woman. And we didn't begrudge her that bed for a second – she deserved it. On the basis of my own experience, I reckoned she'd need about four or five days in Los Arcos before she'd be fit to be on the move again.

Meanwhile, Myron and I moved on through the town and came across a refugio that appeared to be run by a bunch of Austrians. Following the usual ablutions and ritual bagging of bunk and sorting of gear, not to mention drinking more gallons of water, we headed off into the main square of the town to find the action. It was a glorious evening, warm and balmy, picturesque beyond imagining, but neither of us felt remotely like wandering into the church for a holy moment; instead we flunked down at a table under a sprawling white awning and ordered beer – large ones. Before long we were joined by Brian, our fund manager from California, and Katrine, whom I now recalled I had also abandoned to her own devices some time back when she had stopped to nurse her blisters. We were also soon joined by Will, our student friend, and there followed a hugely convivial evening of food, stories and more beer. The old men around the table felt it our duty to try to matchmake Katrine and Will but our best efforts were miserably unsuccessful and all we got from them was a fed-up look as we realised we were being embarrassing.

CHAPTER 16
Unexpected Encounter

The next morning I headed out of Los Arcos alone with the sun slowly rising behind. About a mile out of the town on a road that must have been Roman because it was as straight as could be, I came across Brian. He was in a filthy mood, seething with outrage and indignation. 'Do you see that?' he asked me, pointing at the ground in front of us. In the gloom I noticed what was enraging him. There was excrement in the middle of the track – a reminder of the occasional wretchedness of human nature. What possesses someone to do such a thing? Why would a pilgrim have such disdain for his or her fellows?

Before I knew it I was on the outskirts of Logroño and the big city came as a shock to the system. The noise of the traffic was bad enough, but the urban sprawl of factories, warehouses and out-of-town shopping malls broke the spell of the Camino. But I meandered through it all, over little pedestrian bridges and through tunnels specially constructed for the pilgrim hordes, all the while little yellow arrows keeping me on the right track.

Once in the medieval town, I headed for the municipal refugio where, even at an early hour in the mid-afternoon, there was a queue of people waiting to check in for the night. It was clear that there were in fact far more people than there would be beds and, after the gates to the refugio were opened, a very efficient-looking *hospitalero* indicated where the line would have to be drawn, and a small group of disconsolate pilgrims headed off in search of accommodation elsewhere. Meanwhile, as we snaked our way through the check-in queue, I saw the Italian pilgrim I had encountered the day before. He was wearing his dog as a scarf, the animal limply hanging around his neck. Clearly his pet had not fully recovered from the privations and heat.

Once I was installed in my dormitory, which was clean but utterly overcrowded with at least 60 people in one room, I met up with Brian and we mooched off to see the sights. There are always interesting people to meet and wonderful conversations to have with people sharing their Camino stories. A young couple we met were clearly doing the Camino for athletic purposes rather than spiritual ones. They were travelling the world ticking off walks like birdwatchers adding to their life list of rare species spotted. They'd done a marathon walk through the Rocky Mountains, had been trekking in Nepal and both looked super fit. These two were cracking along, determined to finish the whole Spanish section in three weeks before heading off for a jungle expedition in Cambodia. I wondered if the spirit of the Camino would get hold of them over the coming weeks.

The municipal refugio had a curfew of 10 p.m. All pilgrims were expected to be tucked up in their bunks by then as the lights went out promptly on the hour. Two problems with this arrangement became apparent. Firstly, the man in the adjoining bunk, whose face was inches from mine, was a classically overweight character who managed to lie flat on his back, fall instantly sound asleep and let rip with a baritone snore that made the whole dormitory quake. In the stifling heat of the dorm I knew I was in for a night of sleep deprivation. Secondly, that that night was *festa* night in Logroño. When is it not *festa* night in Spain, I was beginning to ask myself?

I had the most extraordinary feeling of being a small child again. One of my abiding memories of summer evenings in Edinburgh when I was young was of being sent to bed when it was still broad daylight and the birds were still at full throttle. So also were my older brothers and sister and their friends, who continued to play noisily outside my bedroom window whilst I, being the youngest, was expected to get much-needed rest. Listening to Edinburgh birdsong still evokes that melancholy feeling of missing out on all the fun.

By midnight, or perhaps a good deal later, to add to the discordant symphony, the most almighty firework display began as another saint was remembered for his holy works. It was a grim night as far as sleeping was concerned.

At about 5 a.m. there were stirrings amongst the pilgrims. By 5.30 a full-scale evacuation of the refugio was underway. I had barely slept, and as people banged doors, talked loudly and generally behaved in a quite selfish and inconsiderate manner, I became crosser and crosser. Eventually, I got up myself and wandered into the kitchen. Not only had some of the early risers made a ridiculous amount of noise, they had left the kitchen in a real mess. I was furious that people didn't have the consideration to clear up after themselves. I began to speculate about just why they had felt the need to get up so early. They would, after all, be walking for up to two hours in complete darkness. What was the point?

Then it occurred to me that a lot of people were joining the Camino in Logroño, and the route had just got a whole lot busier. I realised these early risers were actually racing to get to the next place ahead of everyone else and getting up earlier and earlier so as not to be left without a roof for the night. I was determined not to join in such a ridiculous pantomime. I sat down in the debris of the kitchen, took out the little Basque knife that I had bought a day or so before and proceeded, at a leisurely pace, to peel the pear I had in my bag and luxuriate over every mouthful.

When I set out that day the foul habits of some of the pilgrim community seemed more noticeable than ever. Whilst I only came across the one poo, all the way along the Camino there are little tissues, deposited where people have squatted for a pee. There are also sweet wrappers and a steady trail of detritus left in the wake of these pious pilgrims. I was determined to be a tidy pilgrim.

Being in La Rioja, it was natural to find vineyards everywhere. On the way out of town, I passed the Italian man with the dog. He was asleep by the side of the trail, his faithful curly-haired companion slumped beside him. He had probably had a better night's sleep than anyone, courtesy of the fact that hardly any refuges accepted pets. He was certainly in no rush to move on. I rather envied him.

I realised that I was in a bit of a mood with my fellow pilgrims. It was probably attributable to sleep deprivation, but I was feeling disappointed by their appalling personal habits. The loos back in Logroño had been left in a terrible state and the woman in the next bunk had left her paper sheets on the bed, in spite of the huge signs in about five different languages instructing people to place them in the receptacle provided for the purpose.

All of this was not helped by poor signage on the way out of Logroño, and the only thing that consoled me was the discovery of how delicious the ripe grapes of the vineyards of La Rioja are. That was my second breakfast. The vines were groaning with fruit and the grape harvest had begun. All along the trail little clusters of pickers had appeared; tractors and trailers were soon passing by laden with this year's produce.

It inspired me to do something to lift my mood. I had my mobile phone with me so, for the first time since I had set off from Le Puy-en-Velay I listened to music. The random selection proved to be just right, and I wondered if the phone had some kind of mood sensor and knew what to play to cheer me up.

I looked again at the trail of pilgrims stretching out for miles ahead: people from all sorts of places and backgrounds with a variety of needs and expectations, but almost all filled with some sense that this journey would be good for them in some way. They were here to explore who they were, to meet others, to take time out of their daily lives in order to reflect and take stock. And so, from feeling grumpy and antagonistic, I was overwhelmed with a deep compassion for my fellow humans. I wanted to applaud all these people who were taking seriously an age-old tradition to walk, and in walking, to open themselves to the world around them, to the people they would meet and to the ways in which this thing we call the Camino might shape and challenge them.

By late morning I arrived in a tiny village called Ventosa. Here I stopped for a cup of coffee and indulged myself with a tortilla sandwich. I felt I deserved it after about 18 kilometres fuelled by a pear and some grapes. The idea of a tortilla sandwich seemed like a good one and I decided that from now on this would be my breakfast of choice.

Feeling fortified and recharged, I set off, and after a short distance I came across an area next to the Camino where people had piled up little mounds of pebbles. I marched on past. I had seen plenty of these little shrines along the way already. It was clearly a custom for people to remind the world they had been this way or to remember loved ones and perhaps to put up a little memorial to someone.

I carried on walking for about 50 yards before I felt a sudden and quite overwhelming urge to turn back and explore that place further. This was very strange and out of character for me. Normally I never go back. Psychologically, when you are on the trail it can sap morale if you have to retrace your steps (like the times I'd had to about-turn to retrieve the stick), but on this occasion I almost felt that I was not really in control. It was as if I was unconsciously obeying some inner command.

I walked back and began to wander amongst the piles of pebbles. I asked myself, what am I doing here? I needed to get on. But I was drawn further towards something I had not spotted before. In one corner of the site was a tiny wooden cross. As I moved closer I saw a pair of hiking boots beside it and on the cross itself a small brass plate. I bent down to read the words. They were in Spanish: 'teacher, friend, mother, pilgrim'. Then I saw the word 'Edinburgh'. I began to feel distinctly odd as I read the name. I paused for a moment, taking all of this in, feeling more and more puzzled. Then, as if struck by a lightning bolt, I realised in an overpowering instant that I knew who this woman was. I had not known her personally, but she had been a colleague of my wife Kate's at the school where they both taught. And what's more, after her death, Kate had been asked to fill her role as a guidance teacher.

How was it, that out of all the roadside shrines along the Camino, I had been drawn so inexplicably to this one?

I was completely overcome and shook with emotion. I couldn't do anything else but phone Kate there and then. I got through to her straight away: it was a Monday morning and I knew she didn't teach on Mondays. I spluttered out what I had just encountered. It felt like a moment of miracle and wonder. Then Kate told me that she had company at that moment. She was busy planning her trip to Spain to join me in a few days' time, and with her to help her prepare for speaking some Spanish was her colleague, Mary, who'd given me the Camino stick a few years before. Furthermore, it was Mary who had created the memorial. On one of her many trips to Spain on school trips, she'd always made a point of taking the pupils out for a day walking on the Camino, and the previous year she had put the cross there. I had had no idea about this. The whole episode affected me profoundly.

I tried to reflect on where all the emotion that welled up in me had come from. On a mundane level it was a remarkable piece of serendipity. The chance moment of discovering a connection with home and with the sad passing of one of Kate's colleagues. There was the story of my own journey which was by now already rich with encounter and ripe with expectation of more surprises and adventures. Then there was another story of loss that had found itself a resting place in this obscure little shrine in Spain. The heartbreak of a mother, wife, friend and teacher taken before her time by illness, and those whom she'd left behind remembering her and treasuring her in this way. And, most astonishingly, how I had come across this little shrine when I had absolutely no reason to have been out there looking for it. It was a very personal and mystical moment for me, both baffling and affirming.

I thought about a great figure of the Scottish church, George Macleod, who'd been rebuilding the abbey on Iona in the 1930s. Supplies of wood for the roof had dried up, most being used for the war effort. A few weeks later, having all but abandoned his plans of getting a new roof on the abbey, a cargo ship had been forced to jettison its load of timber – the perfect roofing material – which washed up on the white beaches of Mull, opposite Iona. 'If you think things like that are pure coincidence, I hope you have a boring life,' he is supposed to have declared, adding that 'Whenever I pray, I find the coincidences multiply.'

Before I became a minster, I had spent a year working in the neighbourhoods of Muirhouse and West Pilton in Edinburgh. I had often found a kind of earthy authenticity amongst people there. I had really enjoyed the straightforward decency and honesty of these folk who lived in poverty and who had been treated harshly by the authorities. There was humour and a sense of perspective that I often found engaging and heart-warming; it frequently caught my imagination and won my respect.

Some of the young mothers I had tried to support were only a year or two younger than myself. For them, having a child often meant leaving home. Usually there was no partner because the father of the child had long since left the scene. Yet what they sought was something rather simple and wonderful. They just wanted to create their own home, to care for and nurture their children, to feel wanted, loved and useful. It used to enrage me that the common, automatic response was to judge them negatively.

Kate, too, had felt drawn to the troublesome kids, the ones for whom the classroom simply wasn't working, the ones who had missed out on networks of nurture and support and whose behaviour had proven challenging. She'd trained as a Forest School leader, and now she was in the midst of making the transition from teaching to counselling; she was about to set up her own practice with a colleague. Her training was according to the philosophy of Karl Rogers, who pioneered the person-centred approach.

Over the years, Kate and I had come to see that our work was overlapping in remarkable ways, especially in trying to see the best in those who'd had difficult experiences. In the context of 'person-centred counselling' the onus is not on trying to fix people or on offering advice or solutions. Instead, the purpose is to be alongside people and act as a companion, or a kind of catalyst which might reflect back what has been said by careful listening and enable people to find their own answers within. The point is to recognise the agency and capacity that people have, if only it can be brought out, encouraged and empowered.

I began to realise, as I walked on that day, how profoundly this approach resonated with the way in which I had sought to work over the years. I had never had a name for it, but I now realised that this was the approach I had been following my whole career. It had emerged from my reading of the way in which Jesus had dealt with people, how he'd empowered them to take control of their own lives, asked them to help him, asked them what they wanted and said to those whom he helped that it wasn't so much him but their own faith (or their own recovered sense of themselves as people worthy of respect) that had healed them.

One of my favourite people in my first parish in Perthshire was a local farmer called Fraser Penny. He was a great musician as well as being an excellent farmer, and he, and his musical wife, gave the gift of music to their children. He was also a wonderful storyteller and great company. When he retired he developed a little vegetable garden at the crossroads near his house. It was very strategically placed, and people would often feel obliged to stop in passing and have a chat. And that seemed to be how he wanted it. I remember one of our conversations, when he told me that a few years before he retired he'd been at a farming conference. 'They were talking about "organic" farming,' he said. 'I hadn't heard the word before, but when they explained it, I realised I'd been doing it for 50 years!'

In the same way, I realised what I was doing in my work had a whole philosophical approach attached to it. The way in which Kate's and my different career paths had woven together was the thing that was making me shake with emotion that day. It was as though the Spirit was making an affirmation of our togetherness, not just in the bonds of love that had woven through us and our children but also in the passions that inspired and shaped our daily lives and work.

To have this confirmed in this mystical way on the roadside at Ventosa was more than I could handle, and the emotion just erupted out of me: joy, affirmation, love, shared passion, purpose, rightness. I surprised myself at how tearful I was, and it could have got hugely embarrassing were it not for the fact that providence helped me further that day with an empty road and the space to express my emotions with a degree of abandon that quite took me aback.

I have often felt that this world is filled with things that people might pass off as pure coincidences or random happenings, but I get the strong sense that we have some kind of spiritual antennae at work in us if only we are prepared to tune in. My spiritual antennae were certainly at work that day.

I decided that after a really disturbed and hot night in an overcrowded dormitory in Logroño I would luxuriate in a single room when I reached Nájera. I got there in the middle of the afternoon and found a small, clean and cheap hotel not far from the town centre. I realised that I needed this mental space after the momentousness of the day. For many, it would have been seen as chance, a pure coincidence and nothing more, but I felt that there was something in that moment that I had to cherish and reflect upon. Many nourishing and fruitful encounters are missed because we fail to listen to those messages from beyond the stars that await a responsive heart. It reminds me of one of my favourite quotes from Annie Dillard's *Pilgrim at Tinker Creek* where she laments how mundane our lives can so often be. 'We are raising tomatoes when we should be raising Cain, or Lazarus,' she declares, claiming that life is much wilder and more unpredictable than, in our timidity, we allow it to be. We so undervalue the mental life of humanity and that capacity of love and heart that we all have. It is said that we use a tiny proportion of our brains on our journey through life, and I am inclined to agree; we are so focused on the rational that we fail sometimes to take account of those things that cannot be so readily explained. So much in life comes to us in chance encounters, in moments ripe with opportunity that we are invited to seize but so often fail to take, out of a desire for an ordered, controlled and unstartling existence. The Camino was leading me into this territory of miracle and wonder.

Nájera proved to be another bleak little place. I went off to spy out how to get out of town in the morning. I was rapidly discovering that this was an exceedingly good ploy. There is nothing more frustrating than wandering around in bewilderment in the gloom of an early morning trying to pick up the route. As I explored I came across an advertisement for a forthcoming bullfight. The picture displayed a matador tormenting a bull from a motorbike. It is one thing to pitch a man against a bull on foot – it is a raw and visceral exchange and the matador is clearly very vulnerable and relies on his wits and skill. As ugly and distasteful as bullfighting is to me, the idea of tackling a bull from a motorbike just seemed to be beyond the pale, the odds stacked so strongly against the bull, unless of course the rider were to come off. It was a depressing sight, and with that gloomy thought I made my way back into the centre of town past a succession of semi-derelict buildings. My spirits lifted as I bumped into Myron, who was staying in the municipal refuge and, like me, was wandering about looking for some food, beer and a bit of company. We installed ourselves in one of the local bars, proceeded to down the first beer of the day and another convivial evening began.

It felt good to share the day's story with him and a couple of other pilgrims who joined us that evening. They were genuinely moved by the powerful experience I'd had, and I felt another connection with those medieval pilgrims described by Chaucer in *The Canterbury Tales*, sitting around a table in the evening, eagerly listening to one another's tales and realising that in the stories exchanged we catch a glimpse of the Spirit alive and doing her work amongst us.

CHAPTER 17

Chicken in the Church

The following day began much later than any since my arrival in Spain. In this little hotel there were no pilgrims rushing to be first on the trail, banging about noisily and leaving debris behind. All was calm, and I realised I had slept like a log. Yes, there had been some fireworks let off in the street below by some local kids late the previous night, but not a full-scale riot. Having checked the route out of town the previous evening, I strode off in great confidence and high spirits.

There is a steady climb out of Nájera through a lovely forest. On this part of the Camino you are never far away from the rich vineyards of La Rioja; I am sure the rich, red soil of the region must contribute much to the distinctive earthiness of the best Rioja wine. At Azofra I stopped for a cup of coffee and bumped into a few familiar faces.

Just as my mood the previous day had begun as one of grumpy resentment at the selfishness and thoughtlessness of some of the pilgrim community, now I was feeling much warmth towards them.

Beyond the rolling vineyards, rather unfortunately, the Camino ran for a few kilometres parallel to a motorway under construction. The juxtaposition of the ancient pathway and the up-to-date European motorway network was a source of some reflection. Of more interest, however, was the snake of pilgrims up ahead that now came into view.

A steady line of humanity, people on foot, on the march, covering ground at a human pace and from so many different cultures and nationalities (a great many Koreans, as it turned out, on this day, for some reason). It felt like a protest movement; so many I had met seemed to be on some kind of search for a different and better world and a better life for themselves. Walking has always been a thing associated with protest. When you want something to change, you walk. There is something very democratic, convivial yet subversive, about human beings on the move.

It proved to be a gunmetal grey day, and the carapace of cloud felt like a heavy weight determinedly trying to lower the mood.

I had been reading about Santo Domingo a little. This was the failed monk who ended up as the hero of the Camino. Having been told repeatedly that he'd never make it as a scholastic monk, he turned to engineering. He built the pilgrim refuge that is now the luxurious parador in Santo Domingo, but more significantly he created a number of bridges over the rivers of the area and paths that eased the journey of pilgrims. Domingo was born in 1019, but his memory lives on in the town that bears his name, whilst all the scholastic monks have long been forgotten.

As I wandered through this beautiful medieval town, I emerged suddenly into the main square. It was completely crowded with people. My first reaction was, I have to confess, one of mild irritation. They were impeding my way! I had a journey to make and a destination to reach, and all these crowds were making it almost impossible to make progress at a satisfactory pace. But once I got off my high horse and took in the scene, I realised that I had stumbled upon a remarkable moment. I cannot believe that what I saw next is a daily occurrence, and so I was thankful that providence had brought me into the square that moment to witness an amazing scene.

There were two giant effigies: one, I presumed, of the saint and another of a woman. They were being held aloft by a group of men and women. The rather humble and bent effigy of Santo Domingo looked unremarkable, yet the plinth on which he was borne was of lavish ornamented silver. In the midst of the confusion and chaos, suddenly a gap opened up and some boys began to do some acrobatics. As they tumbled, they arrived in front of the saint's effigy and shouted out '*Viva el santo!*' and the whole crowd roared their approval. A succession of boys proceeded to do the same feat, with varying degrees of success.

Next, the effigies began to move in different directions. First the female effigy was carried ceremoniously into the smaller church on one side of the square. Then the crowd gathered around the entrance to the cathedral. Another gap opened up and a group of perhaps fifteen boys dressed in blue or red berets and wrapped around with colourful shawls lined the path into the cathedral. Behind them a group of older men pulled out some instruments – what looked like small clarinets and drums. As the band struck up, the boys began a cheerful, ritual dance and the bearers of the saint began a slow march into the cathedral. Having witnessed the cavalcade, I decided not to follow on into the cathedral, but to press on.

Later I read up on the cathedral, which turns out to have the most unlikely residents, in addition to the bones of Santo Domingo. Kept in a cage are two birds, a hen and a cock. The story goes that in medieval times a family of pilgrims visited the town (and stayed, presumably, in Domingo's refuge). In the course of a typical pilgrims' evening during which much conviviality would have taken place, the innkeeper's daughter fell passionately in love with the teenage son of the family. Being an earnest young man, he was not about to give into the temptations of the flesh and rebuffed the young girl's amorous overtures. In a fit of pique, the next morning she hid a silver cup in the young man's pack and denounced him as a thief. The poor young chap was arrested. As was typical in those far-off brutal days, the penalty for theft was death by hanging. Now, this is the point where the story becomes singularly weird, for it seems that, oblivious to the plight of their dear son, the parents continued on their way to Santiago. Weeks later they returned to the town to find that by some miracle, presumably brought about by Santo Domingo, the young man, though swinging from the gibbet, was still alive. The news was reported to the local mayor, sitting at his dinner table about to tuck in to two roast chickens. Naturally, he refused to believe the story. 'The young lad is as dead as these chickens on my plate,' he announced. And just as he said it, the two roast chickens came back to life, leapt off his plate and ran out of the door. There is a saying now in the town: 'Santo Domingo of the Way, where the roosters crow after being roasted.'

Remarkably, there are papal letters in the cathedral archives from Pope Clement VI dated 1350 giving permission for a rooster and a hen to be kept in a cage in the cathedral. I wish I'd stayed long enough to go in and have a look at those two fowl. It is amazing to think that for something close to 700 years they and their predecessors have been clucking away in the cathedral precincts. I also wonder if the acrobatics of the youths has some connection to the story – chickens leaping off a plate or something like it.

It was a huge privilege to arrive in the square at that exact moment to see this tradition played out. Santo Domingo was clearly alive in the hearts of this community. But I pressed on. What I had begun to realise was that homesickness, weariness and a general cloud of gloom could very readily overwhelm me if I didn't keep moving on. It is a terrible admission and realisation to discover how discomfiting it can be to be at a loose end. When idling, I was prone to bouts of melancholy.

A few kilometres beyond Santo Domingo, I arrived at the tiny village of Grañón. It felt as though this might be a good place to find lodging for the night, and the local parish church of St John the Baptist provided very basic but convivial accommodation. On arrival at the church we were handed a mat and encouraged to find a place to sleep on the floor.

It was remarkable how, in such unusual circumstances, everyone seemed to know exactly what to do. People were setting out their sleeping mats, leaving a good yard between each other. The ritual of kit-sorting was in full swing, and there was a quiet concentration on people's faces as we got our gear sorted, discreetly changed clothing and gave each other the courtesy of what little privacy and discretion could be afforded.

The church in Grañón is a complex of medieval buildings, and once we had all our kit and bedding sorted, people began to wander about and work out what we needed to do to get something to eat. The village is tiny with no shops to speak of and only one bar that I could make out. Rather than heading out to find a restaurant with a pilgrim menu, we were expected to prepare a communal meal. I was ushered upstairs to a refectory-type space. There were, as it turned out, 57 people staying in the church that night. As people wandered about and squeezed past each other in the tiny kitchen, it began to become clear that there was someone in charge. Our *hospitalero* was an Englishman who was spending a few months 'giving something back' to the Camino. He explained to us that there was no charge for staying in the church, but instead invited us to make a donation. He would use this money, he declared, to purchase food for tomorrow night's meal, just as the meal we were about to prepare had been provided by the generosity of last night's guests. Somehow, in the midst of the melee, tasks were allocated: some were appointed vegetable-peelers, others table-layers, others just hung around, trying to stay out of the way, reading or chatting in little huddles or pretending to look busy.

I tried to make myself as useful as possible. As we chatted and laughed and squeezed past each other, I got into a conversation with a bubbly American woman called Neve. I could feel another one of those instant friendships coming on. I knew I would relate well to Neve. She was open, warm and friendly, and certainly ready to have a laugh.

All was nearly ready, though I was beginning to get a little nervous that our meal was going to consist of only bread and salad, copious quantities of both admittedly, but after 28 kilometres I felt I needed a bit more than a mound of greenery!

Suddenly a cry went up and all 57 of us were ushered out into the street. I wasn't quite sure what was going on as we paraded along the road to a little shop just a few yards down from the church. There was almost a carnival atmosphere as we were told that we had to sing for our supper. With great relief I realised there would also be something more substantial to eat. A young Mexican man struck up a tune on his guitar. He sang rather well, but just as he completed his song a face popped out from the little shop and declared that whilst this was all very well, they had not heard enough to hand over the food. So a small group of Koreans launched into a traditional song. Again, the lady from the shop announced really we could do better. It was then that Neve shouted over to me, 'Hey, Richard, you're from Scotland, how about a song?' At this point, even though I hadn't had a beer, I launched into a performance of 'By Yon Bonnie Banks'. I am sure it was a tuneless rendition, but it seemed to do the trick: the doors of the shop flew open and a beaming chef emerged with a gigantic platter of pasta and handed it over to the hungry pilgrims. With shouts of gratitude in at least 20 languages, and much laughter and excitement, we marched off back to the church, took our places and began to share out this delicious meal. We tucked into pasta, salad and bread, washed down with the most delicious Rioja. It was fitting, for this was to be my last night in the province of La Rioja. Tomorrow I would be passing into Castilla y León, a huge province that would take us all the way to the mountains in the west.

After supper we were all cordially invited to a pilgrim mass in the main part of the church. I had thought that the place we were sleeping was the main part, but deeper into this warren of medieval buildings was an even larger sanctuary, dark and impressive, where a very friendly priest preached at us at some length, and then we shared the Eucharist. No discrimination here between Catholics and non-Catholics. Later on, we were invited by our *hospitalero* to an upper room high up at the back of the church, possibly a choir loft. The priest had set the place out with numerous candles and invited us to share our Camino thoughts. We went round the group, perhaps 20 of us. It was quite remarkable how a mere walk was having such a huge, transformative impact on people's lives. An opportunity to reflect and rethink life.

Pilgrimage, in medieval times, was often an act of repentance, which simply means a rethinking. Sometimes you wonder how innocent and helpful words and ideas get such a bad reputation. When I hear the word 'repent', I cannot help but think of wild, crazy-eyed Presbyterians wielding their Bibles like weapons. Or the odd serious-minded soul, fearing the imminent apocalypse and wearing a sandwich-board placard warning the public of impending doom because of our sins. Is that really what repentance ought to be about? The idea of rethinking our lives is not about living in mortal fear of the consequences of our waywardness, wary of being struck down by a vengeful, capricious and angry God, so much as an invitation to step back from our lives and reframe them. A certain amount of critical distance is valuable, and where better to rethink your life than on a pilgrimage? How did the idea of the penitential journey get such a bad reputation? It's not about appeasing an angry God or an even angrier church, it's about taking the chance to recalibrate our lives, probably something everyone should try every now and then.

Perhaps the most moving stories that were shared in the atmospheric upper room of this ancient church were those of people for whom the Camino had been a physical as well as an emotional challenge. One woman spoke of the crippling problems she had struggled with. She began her walk overweight, out of condition and having suffered from years of depression and low self-esteem. She described how, for days on end, she'd been on the verge of giving up. But an inner impulse drove her on. She was not going to be defeated by the weakness in her own body, and she was ready to do battle with the demons from her past that had repeatedly told her she was of no worth. Having fought through, she was now beginning to feel utterly renewed, inspired and transformed. This transformation was not just physical but psychological and spiritual too. She felt that the Camino had remade her and given her back a sense of self-worth that had been buried so deep she had almost lost sight of it. It was a story of repentance in the real sense of the word. It was not the grovelling apology to a judgemental higher power that makes us out to be wretched, unworthy sinners – that kind of repentance is the currency of a power-hungry, manipulative church that profits from telling people they will burn if they don't obey it.

Another pilgrim spoke of her recovery from cancer and how this experience felt like the celebration of new life, having been given the all clear by her doctors some months before. Just like that quiet lady back in Massip in France (which seemed like an age ago) she was giving thanks with every step, and all along the way each step was a movement into another stage of life for her.

Sitting in the candlelit gloom of the ancient church, in this village that owed its existence to the pilgrim community and had been playing host to stories such as these for perhaps a thousand years, it felt good to soak this all up. Where else could you go in the world and feel so held by a group of people who had complete respect for one another, so unified as we were in a common purpose? Where in the world could you go and feel so connected to a way of being, a habit and tradition that could work its magic as effectively for a medieval peasant as for a twenty-first-century urban dweller, who might be using an app on a smartphone to connect with the Camino, but who found the landscape, the company and the sharing of the journey so healing, inspiring and renewing that they were rethinking their lives and finding healing.

CHAPTER 18

Mind-numbing Meseta

It was an early start the next morning. Somehow, it did not feel particularly tempting to lie in bed in the church with everyone else busy preparing for the day. To have lain until everyone was on their way would have felt like a subversive act. I suppose this urge to be together, even if we were finding separateness in our togetherness, was strong. Perhaps for the first time, I began to see the unity of the pilgrim community which is so wonderfully evoked by Chaucer. Here are so many people from different walks of life whose paths might never in the normal scheme of things cross, but on the Camino all the artifice of rank, status, position or hierarchy, call it what you will, is dissolved and a new community emerges. There was, in our common actions, an unwritten code, almost universally adhered to, that involved certain courtesies about use of showers and washing facilities and tidying up and preparing meals. It was highlighted even more in this primitive setting in Grañón, and I could fully see the degree to which people found that they felt safe and held in this community.

I had read with not a little disappointment some people who deemed themselves to be authorities on pilgrimage and had singularly failed to allude to this deeply spiritual dimension. It has so much less to do with the idea of fulfilling some ecclesiastical obligation and so much more to do with the free space, in which the Spirit thrives, of creating the ground for the Spirit of Life that blows where it wills – and is certainly not the possession of any church – to mingle and infuse this community of travellers into a mystical unity.

As I moved into Castilla y León, the landscape began to change almost immediately. The lush vineyards of La Rioja were replaced by the rolling hills of the Meseta, where, at this time of year, field after field of wheat had been cut to stubble, giving the land a consistent yellowish hue. I had read in the guidebook that this monotonous landscape can drive a pilgrim crazy. There really wasn't much to look at, just endless hills that had been cultivated for wheat since Roman times. Indeed, a good deal of the walking in this part of Spain is done on the Via Aquila, the road constructed to carry the harvest of this outpost of the Roman empire back to its heart.

As I walked I remembered a book I had read years ago by English writer H.J. Massingham, *The Tree of Life*, in which he'd suggested that there were many factors that had led to the demise of the Roman empire. Most people had assumed (probably thanks to Gibbon, who wrote the seminal six-volume work *The History of the Decline and Fall of the Roman Empire*, published in 1776) that the collapse was due to waves of invaders from the east who'd laid siege to Rome and ultimately overwhelmed the empire, leading to a dark age in Europe. Massingham suggested that there was also a series of agricultural disasters that befell Rome. He attributed these to a change in agricultural practice. Throughout the empire, he suggests, peasant farmers who had been contracted to supply Rome became the victims of a shift in central policy. Rather than work with peasant farmers who owned their own land and traded with the empire to supply grain and wine, the

Roman authorities deprived them of their land and put slaves to work on it instead. The slaves did not know the land well and did not tend it in the way the peasants had done. Why should they, after all? They were merely slaves.

I wondered if this had happened here on the Meseta. It might have done, but these rolling hills were still producing wheat today, and the roads built by the Romans were still in use by local farmers as well as pilgrims. Two thousand years on, this was still productive land. Massingham's view was that for the land to be sustained and remain productive it is important to have stakeholders or husbandmen (and -women) who will care for it and ensure its health.

I also reflected as I walked on what it was that had brought the Visigoths and others to the gates of Rome. No doubt it was the reality of hunger and want in their own regions. Climate change is not just a contemporary problem. It was possibly famine provoked by drought or other climate-related causes that drove people to migrate in search of a new life. So did the Roman empire collapse because of a combination of bad agricultural practice and climate change affecting a part of the world well beyond its borders?

I realised that there are quite a few parallels with today. It has been suggested that one of the triggers for the relentless war in Syria was climate change (see, for example, Joshua Hammer, 'Is a lack of water to blame for the conflict in Syria?' *Smithsonian Magazine*, June 2013). Several years of drought in Syria had driven many people off the land and into the cities looking for work and a better life. Mixed in with this generation of displaced farmers was a huge influx of refugees from conflicts in Iraq and Afghanistan. Such difficult conditions are a breeding ground for discontent and anger, and it may be that the seeds of unrest were sown by a combination of drought and migration caused by war.

Of course, no conflict has a single cause, and many would suggest that the interests of those with power and wealth initiate and drive conflict as the guarantee of their prosperity. The desire of the great Scottish economist Adam Smith to separate government and commerce wasn't driven so much by a devotion to free-market economics as by a recognition that the shadow hand of commercial interests, when they get control of levers of political power, can see profit to be made by waging war. There is little new under the sun.

This is what was going through my mind until a twinge in the left foot, probably a hangover from my tendon problems back in France, led me to curtail both my meditations and my walking for another day in yet another *villa franca*. There are a number of these 'French' towns in Spain. Basically, they are testimony to the popularity of pilgrimage to Santiago ever since the Bishop of Le Puy-en-Velay made the journey all those years ago. These little colonies were established by those who'd completed the Camino and wanted to dedicate their lives to supporting others on their own journeys. It is a phenomenon that continues to the present, and I had met numerous people who'd made such a change in their lives themselves. There was the crazy Italian pizzeria owner back in France offering food without cost but making a living nonetheless. It was what Gilles and Françoise, the delightful couple at St-Pierre-de-Bessuéjouls had done years before. They had come to understand the pilgrimage as, in Robert Macfarlane's words, a 'wonder voyage' and had walked 'out of the verifiable, the predictable, the normal and the reliable into that marvellous dream world of the pilgrim', where a chance encounter could welcome a new thought and the next conversation might change your life and perspective forever. The pilgrim world is a world that embraces the new, invites transformation and reimagines the world. So here at Villa Franca Montes de Oca, which means literally 'the village of the French by the hills of the wild geese', my thoughts ran free. The wild goose within our Celtic tradition is the emblem of the Holy Spirit, the Spirit of God that blows where it wills unfettered and, like the wind, cannot be tamed or domesticated. Maybe the magic of the pilgrimage is that it represents an undomesticated, untamed spirituality, and that's what resonates so powerfully with so many people today who have become disillusioned with organised religion.

The place I chose to stay looked a bit too posh for a pilgrim. It seemed to be a tourist hotel with a rather grand entrance and a large dining room. But I was not feeling up to moving on any further that day so this would have to do. At the rather swanky reception desk, the lady immediately spotted me as a grubby pilgrim and indicated that I needed to go round the back. It is an interesting feeling being treated in this way. My guess is that it happens to a lot of people a lot of the time. Whether receiving free school meals or collecting benefits, whether a refugee or an asylum seeker, whether mentally ill or living with some kind of physical disability, many people receive this kind of treatment.

I discovered that round the back, however, there was a plush bunkhouse, all extremely well appointed and organised, clean and very busy. I found a bed as far away as possible from potential snorers. The beds were surrounded by metre-high partitions and there was a handy little lockable cabinet for valuables. It was all very civilised. Once I had washed my gear, arranged and stowed it, there was time to wander out and see who was around. I bumped into an Irish girl called Deborah, whom I'd met before. She was now laid up with a knee problem and was fairly sure that she wouldn't be walking any further for a while. Another whom I'd met before was Carolein, the Dutch woman who had asked me for a drink of water outside Cizur Menor.

I discovered that the owner of the hotel had been on his own pilgrimage years before, and he'd decided to offer cheap bunkhouse-type accommodation to fellow pilgrims. It was a great idea and something that could easily be copied back home. The deal was very generous, as you could eat in the restaurant with the hotel guests and devour the same food, but at a much-reduced rate – the ubiquitous 'pilgrim menu'! But happily on this occasion no 'flan', and the meal was one of the most varied and delicious I'd had so far on the Camino.

A good number of fellow pilgrims gathered around the table together, probably about 12 of us. As usual the conversation was lively. There was Jacques from Marseille, a wonderfully fit older man who seemed to spend his entire life on the move, walking from one place to another. Carolein was there, as was Trygve, a Norwegian former soldier who was friendly but reserved. He'd just come back from Afghanistan. He had left the forces, and it was clear that there was a lot going on in his head. His pilgrimage was part of the work he was doing to process all that he'd experienced.

I was intrigued by all of them and endlessly curious about what had brought them to this point in their lives. Jacques wasn't the first person I had met who seemed to all intents and purposes to be on an endless pilgrimage. What had led him to this? Did he have family? If he did, what did they think of his endless peregrinations? Like the other Jacques I had met back in France, I wondered what had prompted his obvious desire to be constantly on the move. Had he just got fed up 'painting shutters' back home in Marseille? Again, back in France, I had met the overpoweringly gregarious Cédric who, though he had a wife who was travelling in the Philippines whilst he was walking, seemed determined to befriend and flirt with every woman he could find, so long as they were about a third of his age. You get little hints and insights into the lives of people you meet and it is all so fascinating. But what makes people like Jacques walk endlessly is probably attributable to what that man shared with me early on in the journey when he said pilgrimage can take over your life – you never stop, never settle again.

Of course, this is the story of the endless restlessness that infected humanity many thousands of years ago. The Hebrew Bible tells the story of Cain and Abel, brothers at odds. Cain, the tiller of the soil, was anything but settled after slaying his brother, and wandered the earth, anxious that it would never produce enough for his needs. We have inherited his anxiety, plundering, domesticating, commandeering and transforming the planet ever since. In so doing, we have squeezed out other species, frequently ruined habitats, polluted water courses, fostered so much greed and wrought so much harm. The story of humanity is that of the restless wanderer, never sure that the world will provide us with enough.

The irony here is that the real nomads are the farmers. Abel, by contrast, may have journeyed with his livestock following the seasons year after year in search of grazing pasture, but the pattern of his wandering was settled. It turns out that the truly nomadic people are the tillers of the soil — restless vagrants on the earth, constantly worried that there is not enough land or produce. Our soil-tilling ancestors migrated across the globe in search of fertile land, forced to do so for a variety of reasons, including the degradation of the soil and competition for land. The further irony of all of this is that, in the story, God appears to approve of Abel's chosen way of life rather Cain's. It is as though there is a Divine wisdom that knew, even at the time of Cain, that the tillers of the soil will use everything up.

In the morning, the laid-back, supportive nature of the hotel owner meant that there was absolutely no one around with whom to settle up at 7 a.m. I thought about leaving some money on the reception desk but, for some reason, changed my mind and set off, the honourable side of my brain saying that I'd forward the payment by post, whilst the other side took fiendish delight in realising I'd had a hugely comfortable night, a terrific meal and it hadn't cost me a single euro! I've learned in life it is never too late to right a wrong. Indeed, in writing this, I have been prompted now to post my long-overdue payment, with a note of gratitude.

The route from Villa Franca Montes de Oca heads steadily uphill through a dense woodland. It was still dark, and I'd had nothing to eat that morning. One of the guests from the previous evening, Andreas from Germany, was up ahead fiddling with his boots when I almost fell over him in the gloom. We both agreed that we needed some breakfast and thought we might have a cup of coffee at the next café we found. Thirteen kilometres later at San Juan de Ortega we came across a typical pilgrim stop. It was, by this time, a warm day.

I noted that the number of pilgrims was steadily increasing the further west we journeyed. Some had begun their journey on their own doorstep in The Hague, or Paris, or wherever; others just joined in for the last few hundred kilometres and one always felt that these latecomers lacked the 'authenticity' of those who'd undertaken a really serious journey over many miles and weeks.

The café in San Juan de Ortega proved something of a disappointment. Having walked so far on an empty stomach, I was gasping for a *café con leche* and a tortilla sandwich, something that had become a bit of a staple since back in Ventosa when I was first introduced to it. The benefits of such a breakfast were wonderful, as a tortilla *bocadillo* set me up for the rest of the day and it never seemed necessary to stop again to find some lunch. I'd also noticed that I had steadily been losing a bit of weight and that felt very welcome. Instead of tortilla, however, I had to make do with tiny bits of cake, individually wrapped in cellophane – not the ideal fuel for a hot day on the trail.

Beyond San Juan lay the site of Atapuerca, the place where the earliest human remains in Europe have been found, reckoned to be around a million years old. It was a hot, dry, dusty day and it felt like exactly the sort of place where humans would settle. Open, and not too shrouded by trees – forests, as anyone familiar with fairy-tales knows, are full of danger. With long views in all directions one is able to spot threats a good way off. The river close by is also a must for any human settlement.

So often when you visit a site of historic significance like this, it can feel as though one is merely a detached spectator. Culture and history are observed from behind a rope and, here at Atapuerca, there were the usual interpretation boards and a little museum for those who wanted to learn more.

The 'heritagisation' of history is what my friend Simon Ditchfield of York University spoke about many years ago. His concern was that instead of being participants in an unfolding story we become observers of history, a level of detachment that has consequences for the way in which we understand our present and ourselves. If history is something that is 'mediated' to us by the heritage industry, something viewed from behind a rope, as it were, it becomes something we passively consume rather than actively shape. This begs the question: are we participants in a narrative, able to shape the future in the light of the past and perhaps even shape our view of the past by what we do with the future, or are we isolated individuals for whom the past is a foreign country? If our past is to be interpreted for us and we are not full participants in the unfolding narrative of our common life, there is a risk we erode the picture of ourselves we tell.

Just as I had been coming to see that the pilgrimage journey can enable us to be participants in the landscape and not just observers of it, so I was finding that my walking at a human pace, without recourse to vehicles, was putting me in touch with these early ancestors who'd arrived on foot from many different places. The pilgrimage was giving me a sense of connection to the world, to its geography, its ecology, its people and its fragility. I was making my way across this ancient landscape – a tiny speck, a fragment of humanity in a moment of time – but nonetheless, my footprints making a statement of my presence on this planet just as these ancient peoples had done here, even if only until 'the wind blew over them and the place knew it no more' (Psalm 103:15–16).

From Atapuerca there is a steep pull uphill to a *cruciero*, a cross atop the hill, imaginatively named Puenta de Vista, where I got my first glimpse of Burgos, one of the great cities of northern Spain. The sight of the city made my heart leap, as it was here that I had planned to halt for a day or so and head up to Santander to meet Kate, who was flying over to join me for a few days' walking. I now had a decision to make. Would I head straight to Burgos and wait there for a whole day before getting a bus to Santander, or would I find a place in between to stay the night and head into Burgos in time to get a bus up north to the coast?

The latter seemed to my mind the best option, as I really had no desire to hang around as a tourist in any place, no matter how lovely or interesting it might be. I have never been someone who can do the tourist thing on my own; I always feel the need to compare notes and observations rather than just be content with my own perspectives. I also felt so focused on the walking that I didn't particularly want to get distracted. However, Kate's impending arrival was certainly a distraction that was welcome, and my step became much lighter as I headed downhill in the direction of Burgos.

At this point I decided to stay the night 14 kilometres out of the city and found a charming little albergue at a place called Cardeñuela. It was very small, very clean and really rather peaceful. I rested up, read and found myself bursting with excitement about meeting up with Kate. I suppose that I had found during these absences from her that the only way to cope was to shut off and focus on what and who was immediately around. Now that she was due to arrive in two days, time started to drag and the feeling of anticipation was getting the better of me.

The little albergue soon filled up with familiar faces, and I met some new people too. There was a Swedish guy whom I had dined with at Villa Franca and a Canadian girl called Caitlin, whom I had chatted to at some length around that same table. She had spoken about her aspirations to pursue a career in counselling, just like Kate. There was also an Australian couple, recently retired, who were walking together as a sort of retirement treat to themselves.

CHAPTER 19
Deviation to Santander

In the morning, filled with anticipation, I set off for Burgos, eager to get a bus to Santander. I walked along a dirt track by the side of the airport, though not much was happening there. Down the hill I saw a council truck speeding towards me with a great cloud of dust being thrown up behind it. I braced myself for an uncomfortable few minutes enveloped in choking smog, but as the truck approached the driver slowed right down to a crawl. He gave me a friendly wave and passed me without the merest trace of dust from his tyres. It was the beginning of one of those days in which humanity does credit to itself.

I chose to head into town along the riverbank. It seemed like a much more pleasant way into Burgos than the main road. Sure enough, the riverbank turned out to be beautifully looked after, and all along the way people smiled as they jogged and walked by the river. Somehow, the Camino stick, the rucksack and the whole pilgrim 'get up' invited a kind of respect and encouragement from the people of Burgos. They were obviously used to seeing pilgrims, and many had no doubt walked to Santiago themselves; it was clearly an activity that had a place of honour within the mindset of the citizens of Burgos. It felt heart-warming to be part of such a community and the world felt a good place to inhabit as people responded so positively.

I decided to leave my pack at the bus station. I bought a ridiculously cheap small backpack for the things I needed overnight and by 11 a.m. I was on a bus to Santander. The journey through the Cantabrian Mountains was quite wonderful and the outside temperature seemed to soar. It felt odd to be in a vehicle for the first time for many days, but it was in a good cause.

I arrived in Santander, found a room in a neat little pension close to the bus station with a small balcony, and set off for a haircut to spruce myself up a little for Kate's arrival. The woman who cut my hair was delightfully friendly and offered to trim my beard as well. Somehow, in spite of my almost total failure to have learned any useful Spanish beyond ordering beer, tortilla and coffee, we managed to communicate quite well, and I explained what I had been up to. Of course, Santander is on another pilgrim route to Santiago, so she was fully familiar with the pilgrim culture.

It felt so good to be with Kate and to imagine the prospect of a few days walking with her on the Camino, sharing all my stories and hearing about life back in Edinburgh. The next morning we got a bus back to Burgos and almost immediately started walking. It had felt like a rather elaborate pit-stop. It took a while to find our route out into the countryside and on the way we found a statue of Santo Domingo, the 'architect' of the Camino. It was wonderful to think of this monk who, having been told he was not up to the task of being a scholar, had set about creating the infrastructure of the Camino through the building of bridges and refuges along the way. We walked about 14 kilometres to a prettily preserved village called Rabé de las Calzadas and decided to spend the night in a charming little refugio on the square. There was another festival happening so there were young children out in the street making a good deal of noise until very late. We chatted to a couple of pilgrims, including a guy from the US who reminded us both of a friend back in Edinburgh, and a rather exuberant French Canadian who spoke at great length about himself. The next day, as we set off, he looked right through us as though we had never met.

With a glorious sunrise behind us we climbed up onto the Meseta, with its bleak, almost featureless yellow landscape. There were no houses to be seen, just more miles of stubble, which rather reminded us of the autumn fields in Scotland after the harvest. What differed was the heat and the barrenness that made it feel as though we were walking through a desert. It was one of those days when the mind turns to a kind of mush. There wouldn't have been much to focus on, except for the fact that we had so much catching up to do, and it was good to introduce Kate to the little dots of humanity who, like ants, formed a line-up ahead on their spiritual quest, each with a unique story to tell. As we walked, Kate was soon caught up in the Camino community as a random pilgrim shared his life story with her.

In his book, *The Great Spiritual Migration*, the American theologian Brian McLaren says that many millions of Christians silently worry that the 'brand' of Christianity has been so compromised that 'many of us are barely able to use that label any more'. The church down the centuries has certainly been compromised, by power and the abuse of it, by dogmatic beliefs that have led to people being persecuted or made to feel second-rate. I think of the lesbian, gay, bisexual and transgender community. A few years ago, people in the church were still saying – and some still do – that being gay or transgender was a form of sin or perversion. The evidence couldn't be clearer that this is simply how people are, and yet we continue to make life difficult for them, unable to accept that even our sexual orientation is a part of the giftedness of how we were made. What is hard is the realisation of the wide gap between the church and the genuine spirituality of those who express faith and a profound understanding of Christian teaching about compassion and justice. 'The church is not for the likes of me' is what so many people articulate. They simply don't feel respectable or worthy enough to be a part of it, and the habit of churchgoing doesn't speak to them. Will Parsons, from the recently established British Pilgrimage Trust, comments on the organisation's website, 'The Church in Britain desperately needs to find a way to invite people in.'

Maybe the problem is that the church has become too cerebral, too propositional and reliant on beliefs and doctrines and articles of faith, too fixed in its habits and patterns of adherence and the maintenance of its institutional life that globally-aware, digitally-connected, post-modern and 'post-truth' world people just don't get it. There is a hunger out there for first-hand experience, for faith to be a lived reality, not just a propositional set of doctrines to be adhered to.

There is a hunger also for the habits of the heart of faith to amount to much more than just a hymn sandwich sitting on an uncomfortable pew in a church that could do with a lick of paint and a bit of brightening up out of its faded Victorian elegance. I remember hearing an interview with a location manager for the film industry who said that sometimes they have great difficulty finding streets that look authentic for period drama, but the one place they have no difficulty finding is churches that look old. I am the last person to run down our wonderful built heritage. Ancient sacred places have a powerful resonance and can enable us all to connect with much that is timeless. But we also need to ensure that the whole of the church's story isn't confined to telling a story of a past 'golden age' that clings on, pointing backwards in a world that, in the eyes of the church, has become decadent and is therefore doomed to destruction.

Pilgrimage fits the bill for Millennials, for Generation X, or whatever term we wish to use to describe the present young generation, for many of whom the church is just an embarrassment or a haven for pat and frequently trite answers to life's difficult questions. To be a pilgrim you don't have to jump through hoops or sign up to doctrines you'd rather question – you just have to set off! Indeed, that is what the first ever pilgrim, Abraham, did. Ripe in years, he just upped and left Haran with his equally ancient wife, Sarah, and the rest is history, as it were.

As we walked on, I was reminded of how fruitful it is to walk side by side and converse over an extended period. It's the kind of thing we often don't allow ourselves enough time for in our fast-moving society. Those who headed off on pilgrimage in the Middle Ages might have been engaging in some pious or penitential journey. They might even have paid someone to do it for them. (As my friend Martin Palmer pointed out to me, his name, Palmer, means someone who undertakes a pilgrimage on behalf of another.) But for those who hit the road, they'd have found that the destination is really the journey itself, and it is the time spent in conversation and encounter along the way where the Spirit is really at work, rather than in the place of dry bones at the end of the pilgrimage.

In Scotland, as in England and elsewhere, the practice of pilgrimage was denounced, and destinations like St Andrews, Whithorn and numerous other places were abandoned and their relics lost forever. The Reformers followed the lead of

Luther, who wrote, 'Let every man stay in his own parish, there he will find more than in all the shrines' (*Luther's Works*, volume 54). Calvin too denounced pilgrimage as being bound up in magic and superstition, and he also condemned the commercial exploitation of pilgrims.

So pilgrimage today on the road to Santiago and in other places is not an assent to a set of dogmatic principles; it is not even necessarily an act of piety and devotion. It is for many just a setting-off into something unknown. In this sense it has so much resonance with the story of Abraham, who had no background in devotion or belief. Something prompted him to make a move, to set off and see what might happen.

The Meseta, a landscape of dull, undulating and relentless terrain, can certainly mess with your head, but a monotonous stretch can also lead you into times of reflection. It's actually one of the attractions of the pilgrimage. You become, as Frédéric Gros wrote in *A Philosophy of Walking*, 'an eddy in the stream of immemorial life'. If our world is so full of so many dissatisfactions and false seductions, so many uncertainties and false dreams, then escape, if only for a short time, into a bright unadorned world that has not been hijacked by commercialism is surely something to be welcomed. And certainly, many of the conversations I had with people focused around the hope that the walk might help underwrite the different kind of world they were seeking to create in light of the catastrophe of climate change and a consumerist world spinning crazily towards chaos.

Most obviously, the metaphor of journey seemed hugely important to people. One of the single most important questions we ask of ourselves is, how shall we spend our days? And if the answer to that is that life and the human sojourn in it is to be undertaken in adherence to an immutable set of non-negotiable principles set in stone, then that can be hugely overwhelming and bleak. If, alternatively, it is understood as an enchanted spirit journey, full of the possibilities of grace, newness and discovery, then we can be filled with hope. The pilgrimage journey offers just that kind of opportunity. It becomes 'a time of gifts', the words Patrick Leigh Fermor used for the title of his first volume charting the journey he undertook from the Hook of Holland to Istanbul in the 1930s.

The idea of the Divine comes not as a dogma but a spark in the soul, unformed, unarticulated and often barely understood, but it puts a hunger or light in the dark centre of our souls and we have to go off on a journey to explore what this intimation of eternity might mean. And out in the green, we reconnect with a world that we have for too long objectified and plundered as though it were a mere resource at our disposal. The testing nature of the physical journey reminds us we are subject to nature, fragile and vulnerable, just like the planet itself. The orthodox theologian Philip Sherrard wrote in *The Eclipse of Man and Nature* that the Creation is 'Nothing less than the manifestation of God's hidden being'. The idea that we should feel free to exploit and harm the planet is to suggest that we have permission to do violence to that which gives us life and is the only medium that enables us to perceive the being of the Creator. Harming the planet is like an assault to the very person of the Divine.

An anonymous quote, which might be from St Columba, has stayed with me throughout all my pilgrim journeys. It is about meeting the mystery, whom some call God, 'in the smell of the bracken after rain, in the buzz of the bee in the ear of the foxglove, and in the eyes of the mule – looking with love on the blundering movements of his master'.

So also, in these moments walking across the Meseta, in the deep and resonant silence of day upon day of plodding through this bland landscape, you begin to listen to your own silence in a new way. The silence, the monotony, the empty-headedness becomes a deep voice challenging our settled thinking and upsetting the pretence that we have found an equilibrium in our lives that will see us comfortably through. The silence, the emptiness, allows us to be filled by something beyond – a deeper wisdom than that which the endless chatter and commentary our day-to-day minds can offer. This may come unbidden to the pilgrim and may well be a shock as the journey takes hold of her.

The potential for unsettlement and discomfort is real. Not just the prospect of blisters and tendonitis, but also the discomfort of realising that the life we have been living may not be what we have thought, has about it deficiencies that we train ourselves to live with, and so the pilgrimage becomes a prelude to a change as well as offering the space and time in which to discern what that change might look like. The wonderful Beat poet and wanderer Gary Snyder once wrote, 'Three fourths of philosophy and literature is the talk of people trying to convince themselves that they like the cage they were tricked into entering.' But like the protesters who marched on Washington during the civil rights movement, or those who marched on Westminster from Jarrow during the Depression years of the 1930s, the pilgrim seeks change, which comes not from settled philosophy and written doctrine but from the free-spirited message of the Holy Spirit that comes to us unchained and ready to subvert. 'In any instant,' writes Annie Dillard in *For the Time Being*, 'the sacred may wipe you with a finger, the bush may flare or you may see a bunch of souls in the trees.'

On the pilgrim way, walking at three miles per hour in the green, along paths that countless others have trod, we reconnect and see ourselves as a part of the natural world, not set over it as masters. As the Psalmist puts it, 'The Heavens declare the glory of God and the firmament declares his handiwork' (Psalm 19:1).

For Kate and me, walking has been a huge feature of our life together. Often we walk in the same places, becoming so familiar with them that we witness the changing seasons and how the landscape, or even an individual tree, welcomes its times of dark, winter deadness (a time to regroup and rest), as much as the same tree will erupt in a riot of green in the spring that feels like a festival.

Those few days of sharing the pilgrimage with Kate were very special.

CHAPTER 20
Poisoned Food – Poisoned Relationships?

After two days' walking, Kate went back to Scotland. The night before she left we had checked into a little hotel in Castrojeriz. As she headed off, she was clearly under the weather, and it turned out that she spent the entire journey home throwing up. I started to feel terribly low myself. At first, I thought I just feel miserable because she'd gone. But when I got into the refugio I had earmarked, I began to feel really sick too. The bunks were constructed out of concrete. As I lay there in my hard cell I could feel the world begin to spin, and soon I knew that the hotel in Castrojeriz had given us both food poisoning. It proved to be a ghastly night of retching, and I felt sorry for all the other pilgrims. It is bad enough that they have to put up with snoring, but this as well?

Still, in the morning, I walked on and insulated myself from the world, allowing the pace and rhythm of the walk to soothe and heal me. It is amazing how it can do that. Walking, it seems, can cure almost anything. *Solvitur ambulando* is a Latin phrase that's captured people from St Augustine to Bruce Chatwin.

One of the people who'd shared the dorm with me the night before was a woman called Mardi from Australia. Later in the day, when I was beginning to feel a little more human, we got into conversation. I was quite touched that my indisposition of the previous night had not put her off talking to me. She told me she was having some time away. Her work, she said, with disadvantaged Aboriginal youth, was emotionally draining. We got talking about the differences between religion and spirituality. She had been brought up Catholic but was no longer practising. I ventured that organised religion seemed to be declining, and that meant there was a crisis of faith. At this, she stopped me in my tracks and said, 'Look at all these people on this walk.' Sure enough, we could see numerous little groups and individuals up ahead as the path snaked up over the hills. She went on, 'There is no crisis of faith, there is only a loss of faith in the institutions of religion. There is a longing in so many people to connect with something greater than themselves.'

We went on to talk about our expectations of this journey, and she said that in her view the Camino gives people what they need, not what they want. 'There is an openheartedness in the pilgrim community and a thread that unites us. So there's a richness in having contact with people we might never meet in any other place; there's an open acceptance of people wherever they are from, and there is no judgement around. In all our communities we see people who are disadvantaged by a power imbalance, and here you discover that there is enough for everyone.'

Mardi suggested that all politicians should come on the Camino, sleep in dormitories and muck in with everyone else. They could resolve their difficulties over a walk, over a pilgrimage – the great leveller. It made me think of that wonderful quote from William Beveridge, the author of the welfare state, who declared, 'Bread for all – before cake for anybody.' It's the inequalities and the separation that breed misunderstanding, fear and prejudice. If only people could meet, eye to eye, face to face, without advantage or disadvantage, humanity would see how much we all have in common.

Mardi said that walking the Camino could offer something to troubled youths wherever in the world they hailed from. 'Just imagine sending young criminals on Camino instead of jail.' Then she went on to talk about the way in which injuries and setbacks on the Camino can actually be helpful. If you get blisters or strains, you have to tend to your feet and sometimes accept help. People learn to look out for one another and are introduced to the idea of a caring community. The Camino is not a race, and the experience can help people to deal with the pressures of daily life that can be harsh and unforgiving for many. 'As we walk, we move when we can move and rest and care for ourselves when we need to. The ego and the competitive nature of the human being gets in the way all the time, but here on the Camino that is set aside,' said Mardi. It was a beautiful conversation. A moment of re-imagining a world that is lost, and looking for a kinder and gentler way of being.

In the last mile or two of the day's walk, I caught up with three Irish pilgrims: Mary, a real character, full of fun and warmth and a former primary-school teacher; Tom, a quiet ex-policeman from Athlone; and Jimmy, who turned out to be a Catholic priest from Limerick who had been working as a missionary in South Africa. We walked and chatted and that evening shared a dormitory. I was, temporarily at least, a part of their crew, but only temporarily, that much was clear. They were a unit, though it turned out that none of them had known each other prior to the Camino. It was their nationality and presumably their Catholic faith (as well as their walking pace) that drew them together.

A Scottish Protestant minister could well be a source of suspicion, bearing in mind the hostility to pilgrimage in the reformed tradition. Jimmy, I felt, was not interested in engaging with me, and I wondered if he was a bit wary of me. Mary was very open and full of humour, and Tom, well, he hardly uttered a word at any stage. But, in spite of feeling a bit on the edge, I have to say, I wouldn't have wanted to team up in quite the way this group had done. As sociable as I always wanted to be, I also wanted the solitude, partly because – and this was a good illustration – groups have the effect of alienating others.

We spent the night at a convivial and clean hostel, and a few other people arrived whom I'd encountered before. I made the mistake of choosing a salad for my meal. Not only was this a huge error after a long day on the trail because it was hardly substantial enough to replace the carbs burned up, but it also included white asparagus from a tin, which was utterly foul. A pilgrim needs substantial fare. I do love fresh Scottish asparagus when it is in season. There is a wonderful farm at Eassie, on the Perthshire–Angus border, that is a bit of a pilgrimage spot for us in the early summer when the asparagus is in season.

The next morning I set off after a very large and very stale croissant and the usual *café con leche*. The alcohol of the previous night had put me out of sorts with the world and I made a wrong turn at Sahagún and ended up on the wrong side of a river. Jimmy appeared on the other side and rather smugly looked to be enjoying my misadventure. 'The blind leading the blind,' he shouted across at me, just as I noticed that some other pilgrims had inadvertently followed me down the wrong path. I doubled back and carried on, thinking what had happened was rather an apt metaphor for the way in which, in the past (and occasionally in the present) Catholic priests and Protestant ministers have often viewed each other. There is, amongst some, a feeling that those in the reformed tradition are deviants from the true faith, just as some in the reformed tradition reckon that it wasn't John Knox (the leader of the Reformation in Scotland) who left the Catholic Church in the sixteenth century, but rather many of the popes, some of whom led the most extraordinary lives of decadence with next to no signs of obvious commitment to following the humble Galilean.

When I was minister of St Machar's Cathedral in Aberdeen, I used to tell people I was the only minister in the Church of Scotland to serve under the Pope! The cathedral is crowned by a remarkable medieval heraldic ceiling which includes the coat of arms of Giovanni de' Medici, Pope Leo X. The ceiling dates to 1520 and is a stunning piece of craftsmanship with no fewer than 48 shields representing James IV and many of the barons of Scotland, the bishops of the Scottish church and the kings and potentates of Europe. Leo X's coat of arms is directly above the communion table. He would have been an unlikely religious leader in today's world, but not in the Middle Ages. He was the pope who tried to suppress the Reformer Martin Luther; he led wars and he was a major patron of the arts. On the occasion of his election as pontiff, he was reported to have said, 'Since God has given us the papacy, let us enjoy it.' His predecessor, Julius II, the 'Warrior Pope', had been an even more extraordinary character. On at least two occasions he personally led his armies into battle, though in his defence he also commissioned Michelangelo to paint the Sistine Chapel and spotted and subsequently nurtured the talented painter Raphael.

I cracked on, continuing to feel rather sour about the world. The weather was grey and dismal, just as my mood was that day, and so was the town of Calzada del Coto, which seemed to have nothing to offer the pilgrim. There didn't even seem to be any cafés open. As I walked on through this bleak landscape, the only sign of life was a loud and grumpy dog, thankfully in a kennel, that barked at every pilgrim as he or she passed. It was as if this dog was summing up the sentiments of the entire community: 'Go away!' it seemed to be saying. It was a scene of grim desolation and hostility: the countryside was untidy, the shutters were closed and the land was flat and bleak.

In the midst of my grumpiness, I was alarmed to discern a pilgrim who seemed to catch my stride and shadow me. That's all I need, I thought to myself – some breezy, chatty fellow desperate for friendship. I quietly cursed him and upped my pace, determined to give him no encouragement. However, at Calzadilla de los Hermanillos, he introduced himself. He turned out to be a Norwegian property developer. I didn't really take to him and sought every chance to move on.

In spite of the gloomy terrain, I was enjoying this Roman road and cracking on along it at a good pace. There was a long section of Roman road to Mansilla de las Mulas. There were a few familiar faces in the municipal refuge, a slightly grubby place with rustic amenities. As I wandered through to find a bunk and do my washing, I spotted a couple of American guys I'd seen previously. They seemed very self-contained and didn't engage much with the wider Camino community, but as I worked away at my washing, I realised that they weren't engaging much with each other either. So it goes with the pilgrim community. There are days when it seems that there is not much to be said.

This overwhelming sense of gloom didn't lift for the whole day and carried on into the evening as I shambled about town trying to find a decent place for a meal. It dawned on me that it was Friday. I thought about the Friday evening ritual of home life, a time to draw breath and draw a cold beer from the fridge, a time to enjoy family life. What on earth was I doing here with this shower of strangers in this godforsaken hovel?

Most people at the refuge were self-catering, but this had not been my pattern. Finding that most of the few eating places in town were empty and looked forbidding, and that what shops there were seemed devoid of any fresh food, I bought a few chocolate puddings and some crisps, and retreated back to the hostel to round off what had been a thoroughly wretched day.

Despite my low mood, I had been walking well over the last week or so. I was really tuned into my body and all the aches and pains and blisters of the past were well and truly behind me. It began to feel as though this travelling life is our natural human state. I remember Bruce Chatwin, in his classic book about nomadic peoples *The Songlines*, suggesting that our natural condition is to be on the move and that settling in one place is a relatively recent aspect of the human experience. Once your body is attuned to the expectation of walking at three miles per hour, it settles into a pattern, a sort of 'muscle memory', and the mind is freed to wander and to sink and rise as the emotions erupt from the core of our being. Sometimes the feelings that well up seem to mirror the landscape; a place that feels like a featureless wasteland can turn your mind into something similar, while a beautiful area of hills and woods and colour can enable the spirit to soar. But all the while, you realise that it is the making of space that enables the mind to range with the feet. Who was it that said that he couldn't think without also walking? And the moments of grim, depressing pointlessness should be as welcome as the times when the spirit soars. The depressing ugliness I had walked through that day had found a parallel in the regions of my own mind. It is surely not healthy to suppress that with manufactured cheery optimism.

I read many years ago about the playwright Dennis Potter, who suffered many years of painful psoriasis. As I mentioned before, he discovered in the midst of what he called the 'ache of life' that if he focused on the pain, it could offer him a kind of unexpected clarity beyond the darkness, 'a widening chink of light' through which he could look and take comfort. Seeing into, through and beyond even the grim things of life is profoundly important. Sometimes it is important to name the silences, to give voice to the despair, to utter what is often unutterable.

There is a very profound story in the Hebrew Bible about a day when the Jewish people are utterly overrun by the Philistine army. The Ark of the Covenant, the symbol of Hebrew identity, is captured and it is a day of complete defeat for the people of Israel. A nameless woman gives birth and names her child Ichabod, which means 'glory has departed'. 'You can't call him that,' protest her friends, but she insists, thus helping others to see that there are times when people need to tell it like it is, to plumb the depths, as it were.

As I wandered down the road, I spotted a couple of fellow pilgrims settling down in a café for some refreshment. As I passed, I heard one of them say to his companion, 'Jeez, Gerry, they say we all have doppelgängers, but I didn't think I'd come on the Camino and see yours.' He was obviously referring to me. I smiled to myself as I wondered what kind of mischief I could get up to and lay the blame on Gerry!

As I approached the city of León, there were suddenly roads and cars to be negotiated. As I've said before, this always comes as a shock. As a traveller on foot, humanity's natural method of locomotion, you notice with a fresh clarity just how dominant and aggressive the internal combustion engine is. I enjoy a well-engineered car and have owned a few growlers in my time, but the utter dominance of the car renders the city a hostile environment for the pedestrian. It was the angry priest Ivan Illich who coined the phrase 'convivial tools' for devices and machines that make communal life better. That day I felt the motor car was not one of them!

On the way into León, I came across another scourge of modernity, and a rare sight on the Camino – a supermarket. I wandered in anyway and bought a box of Weetabix. It felt good to have a supply of some decent, familiar carbohydrate on board and it seemed to be exactly what my body was craving, especially after meals of salad, tinned asparagus and chocolate pudding. As I sat by a busy road and guzzled a few bars lubricated by some drinking yogurt, my spirits began to lift. Maybe it wasn't just the landscape and the irritating people I'd come across in the last day or so that had put me into a pit of despair; maybe it was a lack of comforting and nutritious food. Chocolate pudding may be good for a sugar rush, but it doesn't lift you out of a slough of despond.

I found my way to the convent that a few people had recommended as the best place to stay and then set off around the city. It was a Saturday and there was a market in full flow on the street outside the cathedral. I had read somewhere that there had been constant structural problems with the building since construction began in the twelfth century.

Parts of it had had to be rebuilt and shored up over the years. Poor choice of stone was one reason, the fact that the whole site is built on the foundations of a Roman bath complex was another, and there is so much stained glass the walls have always been too weak to hold up the roof properly. But, along with Burgos and Santiago itself, this is an extraordinary feat of Gothic architecture gone mad.

Another interesting site is the basilica dedicated to St Isidore, the sixth-century Archbishop of Seville whose remains were transferred to León during the time the Iberian peninsula was under Moorish control. As I wandered into the basilica, I noticed two elderly priests who were clearly coming to the end of saying mass. As I watched this ritual activity in a church almost empty of worshippers but with a small number of wandering tourists, I spotted one of the priests downing the remains of what looked like a generous helping of communion wine. Out in the square a few minutes later, I saw the same chap wandering off down the street; I am sure he swayed slightly as he went, but maybe not.

I found another square where a small stage had been set up and a rock band had begun a free concert. After a while listening to that and absorbing the contrasts of the day, I headed back to the nuns. In the dormitory I got into conversation with an intriguing former Hare Krishna devotee who came from Wales and ran a very similar enterprise to our furniture workshop at the Grassmarket Community Project. It is such a joy to meet so many people who lead unconventional lives.

I had decided to skip the pilgrim mass in the chapel and turn in early, but it wasn't to be. Just as I wandered shirtless through the dormitory towards the washrooms, I was confronted by a nun in her full habit. She was quite insistent that I should join the evening mass that was about to begin.

She was utterly unflustered by my state of undress, and it seemed ungrateful to refuse, having been offered refuge in this nunnery. So I dutifully got dressed again and headed for the chapel.

The same nun began proceedings, speaking in very clear and articulate Spanish, some of which I was able to follow. She seemed to have a wonderful sense of humour too. Then a young nun, who seemed to have been chosen for her ability in English but not her cheerfulness, read out a dirge-like welcome to the pilgrim community – something, I reflected, that may well happen every night of the year, so I suppose her lack of enthusiasm could be excused. Then the nuns sat meekly to one side, warbled a few tuneless psalms and made way for a decrepit old priest to shuffle in and say mass. At one point he appeared to be struggling to put on his cope. One of the nuns dutifully walked over to help and the mass proceeded with much fiddling, bowing and pouring of various liquids into chalices. The passivity on the part of women within the liturgical traditions of the Catholic Church was really beginning to get to me.

Any thought of an early night had been chased away by my reaction to the mass, and I headed out once more into the streets of León to see what was going on. A few blocks away I came across the most enormous procession. People dressed in elaborate medieval costumes were parading down the main street in front of Gaudí's magnificent town hall. They were, I fear, celebrating the purging of the Moors from Spain. There is no escaping the bloody history of the Christian empire. Pluralism, tolerance, multiculturalism and gender justice have been and continue to be a long way from being achieved in the modern world.

For the first time on the Camino I was offered a free

breakfast by the nuns, and then just outside in the square a woman from New Zealand approached me in the early morning gloom and asked if she could walk with me for the first few miles that day. She said that she was a little nervous about going alone through the streets of León. It was the first time I had come across anyone expressing anxiety about their personal safety on the Camino. But I was happy to oblige and we headed off together.

We walked past the huge edifice of the León Parador. My New Zealand companion told me that the night before last she had stayed there in considerable comfort, and at considerable expense. I experienced a little twinge of jealousy, but soon overcame it. These paradors had once been cheap refuges for the pilgrim community but had slowly been gentrified and were now beyond the pocket of the average pilgrim. They no longer formed any meaningful part of the pilgrim community beyond being ornaments to a glorious past. Today, the pilgrimage infrastructure continues to reinforce its democratic vision, even if the paradors are no longer part of it.

One of the great revelations of the Camino experience was the fact that there were almost no divisions of class and no opportunities for some pilgrims to get privilege for themselves by using money, power or influence. The Camino was turning out to be a glorious leveller. We were only differentiated by the pace at which our legs would carry us. Snoring together in these vast dormitories you could be snoozing beside a baron of industry or a cobbler. With just a few exceptions, I almost never came across any snobbishness or superiority on the Camino; it was refreshing, and it felt that was how humanity ought to be. I also realised as we walked that I was gradually getting used to the snoring and had actually slept well the previous night. There was a definite spring in my step that day.

Thirty-seven kilometres later, I found myself in a place called Hospital de Órbigo. Along the way, I'd heard church bells calling the faithful to Sunday worship. I had been quite alone for large parts of the day and, in the distance, I caught my first glimpse of the mountains that would lead me to Galicia. For the first time on the journey, I had begun to see that this walk might after all have a foreseeable end and that within another week or so I might actually have completed something quite big.

The village of Órbigo has the most wonderful Roman bridge set out over a number of elegant spans across the river. It has obviously been restored but this gives the place an air of timelessness. The whole town seemed to be devoted to the pilgrim community, and there were a number of familiar faces and some new ones to meet. One of the people I had met before but hadn't seen for some time was my American friend Neve, whom I had last seen in Grañón. It was a jolly evening once again, and Neve informed us of her plans to bring some of her children on the Camino next year.

It turned out that Neve had a huge collection of children, some her own and others that she and her husband, who seemed happy to remain at home, keeping house, had adopted. She described in detail how she home-schooled her children. With her quick wit, huge heart and generous demeanour, I came to think of her as quite an exceptional individual. At the end of the table, my three Irish friends made a quiet confederacy (or so my slightly paranoid mind surmised), whilst at the other end, lubricated by generous amounts of good wine, Neve and I and a few others made raucous conversation.

CHAPTER 21

Into the Mountains

The next morning I set off with another lady from Australia called Janette. Unlike Mardi, whom I had met a few days before and was walking to create some headspace for herself away from her intense work with disadvantaged Aboriginal children, Janette, who told me she was soon to be 70, was having a break from her time as a masseuse in order to rest her hands and come to terms with entering her eighth decade. In the gloom of the morning, under a frosty sky, we stumbled around and got slightly lost. Janette explained to me that as she got older she needed to rest more. Years of doing therapeutic massage had taken its toll on the tendons in her hands, and every year, she said, she had to stop for at least a month in order to avoid them seizing up completely. I must say, I was really impressed by Janette. She certainly didn't walk like your average 70-year-old, and she told me that her children and grandchildren had been alarmed when she announced she was heading off to Spain to walk to Santiago. They weren't so much worried about her fitness as her security. She laughed when she told me that she had just emailed home, declaring that she had never been anywhere in the world that she felt safer.

And, of course, she was right. Not only are pilgrims a genial community of people who by and large look out for each other, but the Spanish communities along the way have had a thousand years of offering hospitality and sanctuary to pilgrims. I guess that they know that keeping people safe is a guarantee of preserving the income they make from the pilgrims. If the Camino ever got a reputation for mugging and robbery, I would imagine the numbers would abruptly tail off.

In Astorga, I realised that the mountains I had seen a day or so before were now looming large. The nights were getting cold, and I had next to no warm clothing. It seemed like months ago when Jon had trimmed down my kit and ordered me to send home surplus clothing. Now I needed to find something warm to wear, especially in the early morning. I found a shop close to the main square and bought a rather bizarre, shiny fleece jacket, the only type in stock, and a pair of gloves. The shop was run by an English lady who had come to Astorga in 1972.

Suitably kitted out, I headed up into the hills. Not far along the way, I ran across a young woman who had stayed at the same refugio as me the night before. Eugenia was a student from Greece. She was almost exactly the same age as my oldest son, Will. We chatted easily about a whole range of subjects. Her English was excellent and she also seemed to have a good grasp of Spanish. As we talked I discovered that she spoke Italian too. Walking together through the heat and through a beautiful woodland on what was clearly a very ancient path, we decided to switch to speaking in Italian. For once I felt that I was making an effort as opposed to the usual assumption that everyone could speak English.

At this point I completely surprised myself. The exposure to Spanish and the many other languages I had been hearing had rekindled my capacity with Italian, and although I had not spoken the language much in recent years, time just melted away and I found myself able to converse quite easily. One of the things I had read before I began my walk was that there is no such thing as a mundane conversation on the Camino. I think what I was now discovering was that I knew what I wanted to say; I had things to communicate and ideas to hear from others, and this brought a clarity to speech and listening. Communication, even in a language I had not spoken much in 30 years, became almost effortless. Perhaps, in the past, I had floundered with Italian simply because I was struggling to have anything to say.

As we walked, Eugenia told me of the plans she and her boyfriend had made to come and establish a pilgrim hostel, a refugio, here in Spain. Her boyfriend ran two family businesses back home. One was a café that had been owned and run by his parents for years. The other was a small independent fashion clothing shop he had started up a few years before. The financial crisis of 2008, with the Greek economy in freefall, had meant that in order simply to earn enough he was working all hours. It was exhausting and clearly unsustainable, not to mention the strain it must have been putting on their relationship. One day they were going to break free and do something they both believed in.

What came across so movingly and profoundly was Eugenia's conviction that the way of the Camino had become for her a symbol of an alternative way of life that she now wanted to put all her energy behind. It represented a kind of protest against all the consumerism and mindless materialism that was causing so much grief, especially for the young, all across Europe, in the aftermath of the financial crisis. 'Anyway,' she said, 'the economists are saying that it will take 50 years for the Greek economy to get back to the place we were at in 2007. We have to find alternative ways of living well that don't rely only on making money. The people in charge have screwed it up for our generation.' For me, that was as compelling a reason as any for seeking an alternative way of life.

Eugenia, like so many young people today, was a spirited, articulate and thoughtful individual. She and others of her generation in Greece had experienced so much loss and heartache already in their lives: the humiliation of soup kitchens being set up in formerly prosperous neighbourhoods; the loss of businesses, homes and livelihoods; the indignity of people who'd worked for decades being stripped of their pensions and any hope of a comfortable retirement; and the breathtaking levels of unemployment that particularly affected the young. All of this was happening in the heartland of the great European experiment. It was the same old story – the young and the most vulnerable were shouldering the greatest weight of the burden that had been caused by a crisis that they had next to nothing to do with creating.

As we talked we climbed up into the hills with beautiful views over tree-clad mountains. We were never far away from the ubiquitous wind turbines that were our constant companions across the north of Spain. But none of them was turning today; the stillness was remarkable and some other form of energy production was no doubt in operation to compensate for the lack of wind. I am not against wind farms, but it is always important to realise that you have to have alternative methods of energy production for those days on which the wind doesn't blow.

It felt like an intriguing metaphor to reflect on. The Hebrew word for the spirit of God is the same word for wind – *ruach*. On one occasion, Jesus is approached by a teacher of the law, Nicodemus, who questions him about his teaching. Jesus reminds him that for all his learning and knowledge, there are still things he doesn't understand and invites him not just to rely on his scholarship and learning but to listen to the wind which 'blows where it chooses, and you hear the sound of it, but you do not know where it comes from or where it goes' (John 3:8). I think what Jesus is trying to tell this holy man is that this 'spirit wind' is so mysterious that we must be alert and flexible in our methods of catching it and recognise that we might even occasionally miss it all together.

For many on this pilgrim journey, something was giving them spiritual energy, but it wasn't any institutional church. As one of my Australian fellow pilgrims had said days before, the crisis of faith today really stems from people's mistrust of the church. They know that deeper realities are there to be discovered, but don't see institutional Christianity helping to reveal them.

Watching these motionless turbines as I headed into the mountains, I was struck by the similarity between them and a church that can often feel irrelevant to many today, as if the unpredictable and mysterious *ruach* is blowing in a different way, leaving the church – the structure created to harness it – spiritually empty. Yet on the Camino it was clear the *ruach* was very much in evidence, simply blowing 'where it chooses' and inspiring many pilgrims on their spiritual quest.

Eugenia shared a remarkable story with me. She told me that a few days before she had woken early and set off from her refugio in the pitch dark. In the gloom she had failed to spot any of the yellow arrows that mark the way along the Camino. She described how an uneasy feeling had crept over her as she walked along a track, further and further from her starting point but always hoping that she might stumble on one of the reassuring markers. As she walked on, her anxiety increased, and it was not helped by the sound of a group of crows that seemed to be cawing at her disdainfully.

As she described this experience, it reminded me of a feeling I sometimes have that birds, especially crows, can pick up on a person's mood. They have a certain knowing look about them and can also be quite mischievous. I remember once in my rural parish in Perthshire, a lovely chap told me about the young crow he had found on the roadside and had brought up as a pet when he was a boy. He would cycle off to school from his home at Wolfhill to the primary school at Newbigging every day, and every afternoon the crow would lie in wait for him along the road and accompany him back to the village, riding on the handlebars of his bike.

On one occasion, the local policeman had been heading out to Wolfhill on a call. As he cycled along, the crow, clearly mistaking the policeman for his young master, flapped out from the undergrowth and jumped onto his bike! Policeman and bicycle ended up in an undignified heap in a ditch by the side of the road. The crow probably flapped off back to his vigil with a smirk of devilment.

Many years ago I read about some research that the German scientist Konrad Lorenz had done into the behaviour of crows and ravens. He had found that it was possible to discern between wise and naïve birds. We have all seen a gathering of crows wander about together on the ground. And sometimes, if a human being comes along or some other danger occurs, the crows will all flap into the air together to avoid it. Lorenz noticed that if a young, inexperienced crow raised the alarm, the older crows would ignore him. It seemed to Lorenz that the crows were, in essence, exercising judgement about the wisdom and insight of their fellows and that the younger crows were not sufficiently knowledgeable about potential threats to be taken seriously.

Eugenia eventually felt so uneasy about the path she had chosen that she turned back and at the next junction chose another one. But still the crows flapped about cawing from the branches, making her uneasy. There were still no signs of the familiar yellow arrows, so once again she turned back, retracing her steps. This time she found one of the familiar arrows which sent her in a completely different direction. As her anxiety lifted and she found herself finally on the right track, the crows fell silent.

Now of course this could be pure coincidence, but I like the idea that the crows were so used to the procession of pilgrims moving through their territory that when one of them strayed down the wrong track, they got agitated. There are numerous stories of birds and animals assisting people in ways that can be quite remarkable. I remember reading the autobiography of the Orcadian poet and writer Edwin Muir. He describes a moment of deep anxiety and trauma in his life on an occasion when his wife was taken seriously ill. He had taken her to the local hospital for some tests, and, waiting for news, had stepped outside for some fresh air. In the darkness, he happened to glance over at a tree not far away, and on one of the twigs he caught sight of a little robin. It was sitting 'looking at me quite without fear, with its round eyes and its bright breast liquidly glowing in the light'. In the midst of his worry that little bird took on an 'unearthly radiance', pouring light into his darkness. He found it astonishingly reassuring. It seemed as though this tiny bird was carrying away some of his anxiety.

Walking by the sea or through the hills we often try to 'read' or interpret the landscape. But sometimes, out in the wild and the green, a strange thing can happen – the landscape and the walker can become one. As you walk through a place and get into a meditative state, you can find the landscape holding you, sustaining you or else interrogating you and asking things of you. The landscape is no longer an object to be studied or assessed: it becomes a subject, a participant in a dialogue. You feel a presence that demands a response and offers comfort and even a sense of companionship.

I guess this is what people call the Holy Spirit. I have long been of the view that when we talk about God we shouldn't think of an 'out there' sort of God beyond the stars, inhabiting a distant realm and watching over us from a sapphire throne. Rather, God is in us, and through us and around us. I believe that the Holy Spirit has been seriously overlooked or at least underestimated and is frequently misunderstood, for it is the Spirit that summons us to awareness, for she inhabits all things if only we lift our eyes and open our hearts. As more than one of our poets have said, 'cleave the wood and God is there, turn but a stone and an angel moves'. There are moments, not confined to holy people, when we can be struck by the startling fact of existence. We can be overwhelmed by the 'tree-ness' of the tree, or the mountainous quality of the mountain or the 'human-ness' of another human being, or the 'bird-ness' of a bird. We might even come upon ourselves with a new and surprising clarity.

The actor Alec Guinness, by his own account, was a lonely child. He was sent off to boarding school on the south coast of England as a young boy and spent many hours walking alone along the nearby beaches. But in his autobiography, *My Name Escapes Me*, he wrote of these experiences, explaining that he never felt entirely alone: 'I always found the sea to be good and sufficient company.' The same could also be said of a mountain, a special place, or even a particular tree or a bird that comes to the table in your garden or always turns up when you are digging or weeding.

Roland Walls was a hugely influential spiritual leader in Scotland until his death a few years ago. In *A Simple Life, Roland Walls and the Community of the Transfiguration*, an account of the contemplative community he founded at Roslin in the 1960s, John Miller describes an occasion when Roland felt very anxious about the wellbeing of the community, which was always very small and vulnerable and never had much money. He was worried that it might falter and fail. As he sat in the garden reflecting on these anxieties, a small sparrow landed on his shoulder and stood there for almost a whole minute before it fluttered off into the bushes. Roland became convinced that this was a sign that he should not be anxious – God would watch over his community. After all, even a sparrow does not go unnoticed, and if it was relaxed enough to rest on Roland's shoulder, so he should stop fretting too.

The next morning I awoke filled with expectation and excitement. The hills I had seen from afar several days before were now ahead, and the day was going to be a long slog to between 900 and 1,000 metres above sea level, up into the hills that mark the final stage of the journey to Santiago de Compostela. I set out early whilst it was still dark. I didn't want to be hampered by companions at this stage because I knew that I had not quite overcome my obsession with getting uphill as fast as possible and creating as much sweat as I could. To have had to slow my pace to accommodate others would have been a nightmare. I felt so fit now, my body poised and ready for anything that the day might bring. I was in a sort of groove in which I almost felt that if I did not walk at least 25 kilometres, I might suffer some kind of withdrawal symptoms.

Temperature control has always been an issue for me whilst out in the hills. There is nothing worse than getting too hot with too much clobber on and then building up such a sweat that as soon as you stop you begin to freeze. Here in Spain I had found that the high-altitude air was still warmer than back in Scotland and that the sun would dry you out before you began to freeze. The other thing that made building up a sweat less daunting was the fact that I knew that I could get my clothes washed every night and have lovely freshly laundered kit the next morning. There is absolutely nothing to beat clean, dry socks out on the trail. I am sure it saves the feet no end of hardship.

The path snaked along a river valley, occasionally following the road and at other times heading away from it on ancient cart tracks. Obviously this had at one time been the main road to Bierzo, and on into Galicia. You could tell that this was a remote area.

Back in the 1980s I had come to northern Spain by car. It was only ten years after the dictator General Franco had died. It was obvious that Spain was just opening up and its infrastructure was being entirely rebuilt, especially in the north with a huge road-building and other programmes under way. Those regions where indigenous languages were spoken had probably suffered most under Franco, who presided over a regime that suppressed local languages like those of the Basque and Galician people. Spain in the 1980s was emerging out of a stagnant period under the years of Franco's oppression into the bright new dawn of greater European integration. Franco's fascist rule, which persisted long after fascism had been purged from the rest of Europe, had rendered Spain something of a pariah in terms of its relationship with the rest of the continent. It was now embracing democracy, at least for the time being.

I continued climbing into the hills and, as the morning wore on, my hunger levels increased. It is probably not a good idea to start a walk, especially an uphill one, on an empty stomach. But just as this thought occurred to me, a striking albergue came into view. It was a ramshackle place with huddles of pilgrims loitering around, some tending to their feet, others managing their kit or sitting feasting at big wooden picnic tables. And outside the main entrance was a table groaning with produce. It was the most glorious and welcome sight. Inside was even more food, and it was hard to imagine there was anything in the world worth eating that was not on offer. I fumbled around looking for my wallet, but soon realised that financial transactions were the last thing on anyone's mind. The message was 'Eat your fill and then, when you're satisfied, consider leaving a donation'. And so I settled down to do just that. I spotted a large flask of warm milk and retrieved from my rucksack the rest of the packet of Weetabix I had purchased a few days before in León. I still had a whole stack of twelve. I smothered them in the hot milk and ate the lot as a kind of porridge. After helping myself to some fruit, I realised just how hungry I was.

I was aware of having lost a fair bit of weight, and even with a dozen Weetabix now sloshing around in my stomach, the waistband of my shorts was still loose. I made a generous donation and realised that the people who ran this place were not just operating a business, they were prefiguring in a very practical way an entirely alternative form of economy: one based on trust, on assuming honesty and generosity on the part of others. It was a kind of 'gift economy', and I wondered if this could only work on the Camino, or if we could imagine the magic of this approach making headway in mainstream society.

Fortified and inspired by this interlude, I headed on with a spring in my step. In spite of the altitude, which I guessed now must be around 4,000 feet, the air was unexpectedly still and warm. For miles around the wind turbines were not turning, and I wondered what people were doing for electricity. The fleece I had bought stayed in my backpack; it was a stunning day. The path was rough but obviously well trodden, and it meandered over the hills until the view to the west opened up into the great bowl of Bierzo. Bierzo immediately gave me the sense of being a hidden place, cut off from the outside world by the mountains that hemmed it in. It has a famous microclimate, enjoying some of the hot, dry conditions of the area further east around León, unlike the temperate, cooler conditions of Galicia. But it also benefits from much more rain than Castilla y León, so it has been known as a major wine-producing region since Roman times. I certainly looked forward to sampling some of the delights of the local wine over the next couple of days.

I had decided to spend the night at a small hotel, thanks to a suggestion by Mary from home, who'd raved about the place. It was in a little town of picture-postcard medieval charm. The owner turned out not to be Spanish at all, but French. We sat outside together once I had checked in. Very soon, he began to berate the people of the town, saying that the whole place was a confection of falsity, that the locals were all hypocrites and scoundrels who milked the pilgrim community, that they pretended to be generous and into the spirit of the pilgrimage but, like the over-restored houses and hotels of this town, were a sham. I began to wonder if he had the same conversation every night with other unsuspecting pilgrims who happened upon his establishment. I wondered also what his relationship was like with the local community, and I also noticed that just as he didn't hold back in his criticism of them, so he didn't hold back in his consumption of Campari sodas, his tipple of choice.

It was a relief when we were joined by another guest. This guy was wearing a cassock, and he had a rather fancy chain attached to his belt that I presumed were prayer beads. It turned out that he was a Dominican friar from Marseille. Unlike some of the other monks and friars I had seen who often looked impoverished and grubby, he was smart, well groomed and had a worldly, sophisticated air about him. If I thought the arrival of this new guest was going to dilute the owner's rage at his fellow citizens, I was very swiftly proved wrong. It turned out that the owner was originally from Marseille too. They were very quickly as thick as thieves. The Dominican also started to criticise the pilgrim community for their slovenly ways, their lack of proper devotion to the church and their anarchic failure to adopt an appropriate attitude of reverence or penitence. He was an angry chap. He declared that he had, by and large, avoided the pilgrim hostels along the way and stayed almost exclusively in hotels. He was soon knocking back the Campari with his fellow Marseillais.

I decided that he represented a religious perspective that needed to be both challenged and set aside. It was judgmental, authoritarian and superior. What is more, he wasn't even prepared to muck in with the plebs on the Camino – he seemed far too aloof. But I enjoyed tangling with him, smiling and trying desperately to keep up with the conversation that switched from French to Italian, for my benefit, when I was no longer able to follow what was being said in French. I certainly wasn't going to confess to being a Protestant minister. I'd have felt like a complete outlander. But it did strengthen my resolve to try to learn French properly. But, more importantly, the conversation also strengthened my resolve about the need for the church to find a new way of relating to the world.

The next day was another high-level walk through stunning countryside, looking down on Ponferrada with its smoke stacks, sitting in stark contrast to the peaceful greenery all around. On the crest of a hill, and quite unexpectedly, I stumbled into the magical little town of O Cebreiro. It's a well-preserved, if perhaps over-restored, medieval town. As I wandered round the streets, I met my priest friend Jimmy, who told me that today was the feast day of St Francis. I hadn't realised. There was a mass going on in the local church to celebrate, but I got the impression that he didn't wish to extend an invitation to a Protestant. After losing Jimmy and feeling a bit excluded, I waited my moment and wandered over to the chapel. There was indeed a service going on and Francis was the focus of attention. I lurked at the back and stayed out of the way. For some reason I didn't want to be spotted by Jimmy.

It is reputed that the saint himself worshipped in this very church on his own pilgrimage to Santiago sometime in the thirteenth century. It felt rather wonderful, as minister of a church that derives its name from the Franciscans – the Kirk of the Greyfriars in Edinburgh – that I should be here on this day of all days, but I also felt the weight of our divisions and that feeling of unfriendliness I'd picked up from Jimmy. It all felt wholly wrong and muddled and all too human! So many differences exist in our heads rather than in objective reality and can probably be settled over a walk together or perhaps a civilised drink at the end of a hot day's walking. I could imagine becoming a friend of Jimmy's, and have indeed counted a number of Catholic priests as good friends over the years.

I made my way back to the refugio. I did my usual evening ritual and noticed the appalling smell of stale socks. I also noticed how closely the bunks were crammed together, and I dreaded to think who I might be sleeping next to that night.

The refugio didn't feel like a place that was conducive to hanging out – they rarely do – so I headed out for a walk, which might seem a bit barmy considering the mileage I had already clocked up that day. But the evening was a wonderful time to be out. There were no other people on the trail, the light was stunningly beautiful and it was also possible to get a sense of the route for the next morning, since, as I imagined, I'd be setting off in the dark again.

Back in town I found a place to eat and my Irish triumvirate showed up. And then, to my delight and surprise, Jimmy bought me a drink and we had a wonderful, friendly chat. If anything, this underlined the degree to which we construct our own narratives about what other people think and what motivates their actions. But in reality we often simply do not know how others feel about us. The fact that I felt negatively judged by a Catholic priest because I am a minister in the reformed tradition probably says more about me than it does about what was really going on.

CHAPTER 22
Santiago, Mata Moros

In the early morning gloom I walked beneath a structure that had been part of the revolution in road-building I had seen the beginnings of on my previous visit in the 1980s. Far above me, almost entirely on concrete stilts, was the new highway that crosses the north of Spain and links the remote area of Galicia with the prosperous east. At this early hour, lorry after lorry passed, entirely out of sight, but filling the valley with the dull roar of engines and the whine of tyres. It was the coldest morning I had yet encountered, and I needed my fleece and gloves in the chill air.

I now had to communicate with Jo, a friend from Edinburgh with whom I'd done a few Scottish pilgrim walks. He was due to join me any day now to walk the last part of the Camino with me. I was cracking on at a fair pace and was reluctant to slow down. But I knew that Jo would want to walk at least from Sarria, which is about 100 kilometres from Santiago. If you do the full 100 kilometres you are entitled to claim a pilgrimage certificate at Santiago.

How could I stall the journey without feeling I was hanging around? The answer came in the shape of the former monastery of San Cristobo. This was a place that gets a good write up in the guidebooks, but getting there requires a detour of about 12 kilometres off the main drag.

I headed off and found the place in the late afternoon.

It had been a monastery until the 1950s, was abandoned for years and recently, with the help of a generous benefactor, had been beautifully restored. It has a number of curious white towers and is set in the most gorgeous wooded location. Like so many of these ancient monasteries, the monks certainly knew how to choose their spot. There was only one drawback. There was absolutely no one about. The place was completely deserted, not a pilgrim or a *hospitalero* in sight. I hung around for a while and began to fret a little about how I could survive overnight on the solitary pear that I was carrying.

I had wandered through the building rather noisily for about 20 minutes, when a young woman appeared. She got me sorted out with a bed in a dormitory that probably had about 40 bunks in it. I asked if there was anywhere to eat and she said no. The nearest shop was several kilometres away. But, she said, if I didn't have any food, there was a farm just down the road that provided meals for pilgrims at a modest charge. If I reappeared at reception at around 7 p.m., she'd show me the way and in the meantime would telephone them to say that I was coming. So, I had this entire swanky monastery all to myself. It did feel odd.

At 7 p.m. the girl from reception appeared and pointed me in the direction of the farm. It was only a few hundred metres down the road with a solitary and rather stark street- light outside the front door, which was rather incongruous in the charming rural isolation of this spot. The couple who greeted me could not have been more pleasant or welcoming. They ushered me into a simple room and sat me down at a table with a plastic cloth. It was all very basic, but I had a good feeling about the place and about these lovely people, who reminded me of a couple I knew from my days in Italy, Paulina and Gigi from the

Kremlino, so called because it was a community-owned bar, in Portalbera.

Gigi was a toothless, gnarled soul who became a great friend during the time I lived there. The Kremlino menu never changed – it was panzerotti every night – and the wine was full of sediment. It made your mouth turn purple but was utterly delicious. And Gigi insisted on giving me a free whisky every night at the end of the meal. Gigi and Paulina became great pals, and years later I went back to visit. Paulina by this time was an elderly lady, but she was still dignified and utterly charming. After about 25 years she still remembered me and told me that Gigi had died just a couple of years before. 'He had a nickname for you,' she said.

'Yes,' I replied, 'he used to call me the blue-eyed Sicilian gangster.'

'No, no, he had another name. He used to call you "the priest".' That took me aback, as this was before I had begun to study to be a minister, and when I explained how I had spent the intervening years, we had a wonderful reunion. It seemed that Gigi's instincts about me all those years ago had been right.

The couple here in Spain were chips off the same block. For them, it felt as though hospitality to the stranger was a sacred duty, even if they didn't have a word of English, and my Spanish was all but non-existent. That night I ate like a prince. I admit I was starving, but the food was truly delicious – pasta with an exquisite sauce made with what I presumed were locally picked mushrooms. It was melt-in-the-mouth stuff. Then there was a beautiful slab of meat with salad and waxy potatoes, and wine that was nothing short of nectar. At the end of it all, they both came into the room. The husband beamed at me and pulled out a bottle of liqueur from behind his back. They managed to explain to me that this was something they produced themselves and that they reserved it only for guests they felt were special. What a way to end the meal. I felt warmed, buoyed and entirely satisfied. Human nature doesn't get better than this, I thought to myself: I left them with warm salutations as they stood at their front door under the orange glow of their street light, waving as I made my way back to the monastery.

I wandered into my dormitory to be confronted by a couple of fellow pilgrims who'd turned up whilst I was out at dinner. To my horror, the man was someone I remembered from the previous night, probably the loudest snorer I had ever come across. I wondered how his partner could possibly put up with him. At 1 a.m., under a thunderous cacophony, I slipped out of the dormitory and found another bed in an empty room. As I settled down again I smiled to myself at how, when things couldn't get better, something, like a snorer, can appear and spoil the dream, or at least remind you that in life, like the rose, there is always the thorn. But the evening's meal and the friendliness of my hosts lulled me into a wonderful restoring sleep.

In the morning it didn't take me long to walk to the village of Samos. I decided that I'd book a hotel for Jo and me there, rather than in Sarria. This was partly so that I didn't have to spend too long hanging about waiting for Jo, who was now due to arrive that evening in Sarria, and partly because the Benedictine monastery at Samos seemed like a good place for him to start his walk. I'd also got the impression that he wasn't too keen on dormitory life. After booking a hotel room close to the monastery, I headed off to Sarria to meet him off the train.

Along the way I met up again with Eugenia from Greece

and we had another great chat. The weather was gentle and warm, and Sarria was busy with pilgrims hanging out in every café. I stopped at one busy place and loaded up with some food. There was a large group of people sitting outside, and they insisted I join them. It was a strange thing, because I didn't recognise any of them, so I was curious why they wanted me to join in. I assumed that they all knew each other, and I felt that I was intruding. Then I realised that none of the people at this table knew each other either, but they were celebrating someone's fortieth birthday, and, as pilgrims together, were establishing instant friendships and helping one of their number to celebrate a milestone. It all felt rather lovely, relaxed and straightforward. There was none of the awkwardness and wariness that generally goes on back home when people meet for the first time. What class is this person? What school did he go to? What are her motives? All that kind of nonsense was completely absent. The world is saturated with the tears of those who have been excluded, negatively judged, maltreated and taken advantage of. We have to learn how to live with more humility and respect, and there's bucketloads of that in the Camino community.

I lurked around Sarria for what seemed like an interminable time waiting for Jo's train. At the station, I found a taxi driver who was willing to drive us back to Samos when Jo arrived. When they announced that the train was delayed, I fully expected the driver to clear off, but he waited patiently until it came. It was great to see a familiar face, and we had a warm reunion. It is always a challenge to invite someone into a mental space that you've been inhabiting for weeks, but Jo was open, enthusiastic and ready to get in step, as it were. I just had to get used to the idea that I was no longer alone and wouldn't be until we arrived in Santiago.

We headed to Samos, and after checking into our hotel we made our way to the vast monastery, one of the largest in Europe, just in time for the pilgrim mass. This huge establishment is now home to only a handful of monks. Vespers flowed into a mass and then, for the first time on the Camino in my experience, came the sprinkling of holy water, a sort of baptism for Jo on the threshold of his pilgrimage journey. There was a sermon, which was as long as any Presbyterian one, and I even realised I was beginning to follow some of what the priest was saying. It seemed to be about matrimony and football. The gist of it was that a lot of Spanish men were more interested in attending football matches than they were in attending to their marriages. Nothing new there.

All through the service I noticed that I was feeling uncomfortable. I couldn't quite put my finger on the reason. It wasn't the sermon or the holy water, or Jo's arrival, but something was giving me a feeling of profound uneasiness. Then I looked up and realised what it was. We were sitting under a pillar in the vast sanctuary and hard against the pillar was an enormous statue of Santiago, St James. Well, that shouldn't have been too disturbing or surprising. What caught my eye as I began to focus was the severed head of a man, a man with clearly North African features, at the base of the sculpture. On top of the African's head was the foot of Santiago, and in the saint's right hand, held above his head, was a long sword. This was a representation of Santiago, Mata Moros, 'St James the Moor-slayer'.

The legend was that in the period when the Moors were being driven out of Spain, St James is supposed to have appeared and helped with the slaughter. It all felt completely tragic and disturbing, and once again I became aware of that thing that might almost be a sixth sense, when we can be unconsciously aware of things close by that we haven't fully taken in. It reminded me of that moment back near Logroño when I had found myself drawn to the spot where there was a memorial to Kate's colleague. The Camino was teaching me to listen to that part of our brains that we so frequently overrule or dismiss.

Jo came with news about my poor dad, whom it now turned out had stopped eating and was near the end. As we walked over the next few days, I had to decide what to do. I certainly didn't want to be here in Spain knowing that my dad was breathing his last. Our son, Will, had said to me on a Skype call that he thought Dad was waiting for me to come home so that he could say goodbye. I decided to walk with Jo to Santiago and then head home. Previously, we'd thought that Kate might come out again and the three of us would walk together to 'the end of the earth' (or Cape Finisterre, as they call it). That was looking unlikely now with my father getting weaker by the day.

CHAPTER 23
Nearing Santiago

The Galician countryside is full of the aroma of cow dung. It is a moist region of small farms and lush grasslands, and it reminded me a bit of Devon. The other thing that resonated with Devon was some of the ancient paths we walked along, in some places several feet below the level of the surrounding land. It was as though the millions of pilgrims who'd walked this way over a millennium had worn the paths down. On either side were vast hedgerows and ancient trees and then occasional plantations of eucalyptus that were clearly a local cash crop. Like so many alien species, they seemed to thrive at the expense of almost every other indigenous plant, so were something of a scar on the landscape.

For most of my walk I'd had snippets of conversation with people I walked with for an hour or so or with whom I sat down to eat in the evening. Now Jo and I were in constant dialogue, and I spent a lot of time regaling him with my Camino story. He was a tolerant and generous listener.

Jo's arrival marked a change in the nature of the walk. A lot of people undertake the Camino in groups of two or three or even more. It can be a wonderful opportunity to share a long and deep conversation that lasts over an extended period. The Camino is also a time for being alone, with odd moments of interaction interspersed with profound solitude. It felt quite different being in company, but good nonetheless. Jo brought a little bit of familiar Edinburgh with him, and I suppose I had been pining somewhat for that. And, as he is so involved in the life of Greyfriars, I got the news of all that had been going on during my absence.

The dynamic of the walk was changing. People tend to leave you alone more when you are in company, as they don't want to interrupt. There is a degree to which the chance encounter, the open exchange, the instant intimacy of friendship can be lost. Walking alone gives you the freedom to be entirely yourself, to encounter people on your own terms. There's a certain confidence and reassurance that comes from knowing that whatever you say, the conversation is preserved in the moment, sealed by the journey. It's the unwritten code of the Camino – the mutual trust and respect of the Camino community who, by and large, recognise that there's a shared sense of confidentiality that comes from knowing you'll probably never cross paths again.

I found myself reflecting again on the power of pilgrimage to enable people to grow spiritually in a time when many churches struggle to make sense and offer genuine nourishment. Part of the reason for this must be that the Spirit is able to come spontaneously amongst a company of strangers. The message that the churches so often peddle isn't an invitation to encounter the Spirit but an invitation to encounter institutional religion. The Spirit which inhabits the Camino community is wild, free and often surprising, and is all the more energising for that. The Spirit that inhabits our churches can be negative, beleaguered and defensive, and who wants to join an anxious institution apparently obsessed with its own self-preservation?

As we got nearer to Santiago, heading west, the weather started to deteriorate, and by the time we were close there was almost constant grey sky and bouts of rain. Passing a run-down little farmstead, a wrinkly old lady greeted us, her feet and ankles caked in mud. She had a toothless, sympathetic smile. My first impression was of a woman carrying the marks of a hard life of physical toil on her face. She looked haggard, yet her eyes glistened with an appealing kindness. As we walked past she offered us a rather limp-looking pancake. I took it, and she shook some sugar onto it and a brief squeeze of lemon.

My first thought was to consider this an act of simple generosity. I had construed an instant narrative in my head along the lines of the story from the Gospels of the widow's mite. The poorest of women comes to the synagogue and gives a tiny offering which was just about all she had. Jesus compares her generosity with the ostentatious offerings of the rich, which, in comparison, had cost them very little. There is a powerful moment in Aleksandr Solzhenitsyn's *The Gulag Archipelago* in which a trainload of detainees slowly chugs past an old peasant woman standing in the middle of a field. One of the prisoners notices that the woman is weeping and constantly crossing herself as she watches the prisoners heading off to hard labour and, quite likely, oblivion. Somehow, this poor woman's faith and compassion becomes a source of strength and consolation in a dark moment of deep hopelessness.

As I was musing on such random acts of kindness, the old woman thrust her hands, now empty, under my chin and I realised she was demanding payment. I had the immediate feeling of having been duped. But I plunged my hand into my pocket, retrieved a coin and handed it over. A few yards further on, I turned back and saw her at it again with the next band of pilgrims. She clearly had quite a business going. Reflecting on this, I didn't begrudge her for the disappointment I felt; it was an indication of just how economically marginal this remote corner of north-west Spain can be.

We stayed for a night just 12 kilometres from Santiago, deciding that it would be good to arrive in time to attend the pilgrim mass in the cathedral at noon. The rain beat down on our last morning and we were soaked through. I had managed to go for weeks without bringing out my ridiculous blue poncho, but I had to retrieve it now from the bottom of my rucksack. It felt fitting, in a way, that the journey should come to an end in the precincts of a great cathedral with the rain battering down, just as it had begun. I suppose I should have been euphoric, feeling a degree of satisfaction, but in fact I felt quite numb. Arriving here meant the end of a journey that had totally absorbed me, so there was disappointment at that, but there was also excitement at the prospect of being home and sleeping in a familiar bed.

In Santiago I felt the pull to get back to my father and my family. But in the midst of all of this I knew that this experience had changed me. It had inspired me, reshaped me and given me so much to reflect on. In spite of my times of being 'empty-headed' as I walked, I realised that there were so many experiences that were going to go on nourishing me, inspiring me and shaping me for years to come. I had found in the physical act of a sustained period of walking, in the connecting with landscape, in the random encounters, in the strange territory of acknowledging my own vulnerability an entirely new perspective on my life back in Edinburgh. Within a few weeks of coming home an observant member of my congregation even suggested that the entire nature of my preaching had changed (for the better!).

That morning in Santiago was spent collecting certificates

and having pilgrim passports signed and verified. There was a fair amount of hanging out in the cathedral square bumping into fellow pilgrims, some of whom I'd been seeing off and on for days, if not weeks. We were a real community, all of us sharing the knowledge of the life-changing experience we'd had, and each one knowing that the experience was unique to them. Then, at midday, we trooped into the cathedral itself for the daily pilgrim mass. By this time the stick had almost become part of me – my indispensable companion – and unlike at St Puy-en-Velay, right at the start of my journey, it behaved itself and didn't threaten to disappear through a grating into the bowels of the church.

In the cathedral there must have been close to a thousand pilgrims. There was standing room only. In the chancel a cluster of priests gathered, some who had just arrived at the end of their own pilgrimages and others who were local clergy and must have done this kind of thing every day of the year. An elderly nun warbled a song, a few platitudes were spoken and then we all got a chance to receive communion.

At the end of it all, the thing everyone wants to see happened: the *Botafumeiro* was lit and was swung across the cathedral from transept to transept. What a sight it was. This colossal incense-burner was the size of a large man, and there were a group of about half a dozen vergers who hauled on a pulley to get the thing going. It was a real art and the vergers set about their task with relish and skill. Great clouds of smoke belched from its innards as it gathered momentum and whooshed from side to side across the cathedral. It looked for all the world like a health-and-safety nightmare, the sort of thing that would be banned in Britain. If anyone had got in the way, there is no doubt they would have been killed. Indeed we heard that on one occasion many years ago the rope had snapped and the *Botafumeiro* had launched itself at a cluster of hapless pilgrims, killing several of them outright. What a way to end a pilgrimage.

Thankfully, that day, the whole event passed off without incident. Maybe it was because I was preoccupied about getting home to see my dad, or maybe it was because I had been so absorbed by the journey and all it had given me, that its completion felt something of an anticlimax. Celebration didn't seem to be in order, and somehow, though I'd often taken a delight in receiving communion at any time, but especially recently in a Catholic church, I didn't get anything much out of this moment, though Jo was good and reassuring company.

It was an ending, but it didn't feel like a spiritual experience, unlike so many of the encounters I'd had along the way. I couldn't quite work out my emotions on this day of all days. As we stood watching the crowds of pilgrims ending their journey in this ecclesiastical setting, I wondered what constituted a fulfilling worship experience and why I wasn't inspired by this one.

Once, with members of our Grassmarket Community Project and others from our association of Old Town Churches, we went on a pilgrimage to Perthshire. We visited the ancient cathedral of Dunkeld and attended the morning service. From there, we walked along the banks of the River Tay through Birnam Wood and saw some of the ancient oaks made famous by Shakespeare in Act IV of *Macbeth*, where the witches predict that Macbeth will never be defeated 'until great Birnam wood to high Dunsinane hill shall come against him'. From there we travelled to the hill of Dunsinane itself (or Dunsinnan, as it is commonly known today in the district) and ended our day at Collace Church, an ancient Celtic sacred site, just at the foot of the hill and the place where I began my life as a parish minister. At the end of our pilgrimage I celebrated a very informal communion service, very different to the one I experienced in Santiago.

I had been reluctant to get too formal in the communion because I knew that for some of the people there, this was the first time they had ever been to a church service, let alone taken communion. I wanted them to feel comfortable and reassured that they were not unworthy or unwelcome. So instead of conducting a formal celebration, I simply told the story of Jesus's last night with his disciples in my own words. Then I took a piece of bread and broke it and asked people to break a piece and share it with their neighbour. I then invited them to take a sip from the earthenware goblet I had brought for the wine.

There was a brief moment of awkwardness when I saw one of our group looking puzzled about what he was supposed to do. A woman called Elizabeth, who was sitting next to him, gave him a little word of reassurance and encouragement. 'Just break a piece off and eat it and then pass the bread on,' she whispered. For me, this was a powerful and moving moment. Elizabeth was someone I had known for many years. When she first came to the Grassmarket Community Project she was profoundly shy, had almost no confidence and was paralysed by her own lack of self-esteem. Over the years I have seen her grow in stature and become more confident and proud of herself and what she is capable of. She is a remarkable and wonderful human being. That day, to see her take the initiative and put another person at their ease, giving them confidence to participate, was really special.

In so much of my life, like that day in the cathedral at Santiago, I have seen and shared in liturgies that have often felt contrived and intimidating for those unfamiliar with church ritual. I felt ungenerous in having such thoughts – for many of those present this would have been a profound and moving occasion, the culmination of weeks of walking and the overcoming of personal challenges. But I was becoming more and more attuned to those moments that the ritual of a church service only point to, moments when love, kindness, generosity and deep, authentic, human connection become the currency of the exchange. The ritual points us in the direction of making these things real in the life we live, but we so often fall short. I was coming to see that some of the transforming moments I had been privileged to witness in my ministry, especially with those who'd been half broken by life, and some of the moments I had shared along the Camino way, had a deep and moving authenticity of which the liturgy of worship is but a shadow. In this sense, the ritual of worship is always pointing away from itself to life outside the walls of the church where kindness, gentleness, compassion and friendship have the power to reimagine the world. As someone once said, 'The real liturgy happens outside the church.'

There is a wonderful coda to the communion story in Collace Church that came to me a few weeks afterwards. Bob Gould, a Canadian non-stipendiary Episcopal priest and friend who'd been with us that day, said that he and others from his church had been caught out by the fact that the liturgy did not seem to have started in any obvious way. At first, he explained, it almost felt as though this was a failure of good order (and of course, there is in the church, especially the Episcopal Church and some branches of the Church of Scotland, something of an obsession with proper liturgical practice). However, Bob's second thought was that what had happened that day, when he had been taken unawares, thinking that the service hadn't really begun, was probably much more in line with what had happened on that first night in the upper room, when, at the end of a Passover meal, Jesus suddenly took a loaf of bread and broke it and shared it with his disciples, telling them that the bread was like his body, broken for them, and that the wine he shared with them was the emblem of his blood about to be shed. They were probably quite unprepared for this act, and it certainly wasn't a formal ritual. The impact and subversive resonance of what happened was all the more powerful for the fact that it carried with it a degree of spontaneity, leaving space for the Spirit to do her own thing. The surprise of the sacred is what the Camino has helped me to look for and, though I continue to love leading worship and crafting sermons, I find myself increasingly enriched by those unanticipated moments rather than the staged formalised ones that happen in church.

I will never forget the lectures given by Andrew Ross, who taught ecclesiastical history at New College in the University of Edinburgh whilst I was a student there. He had been a missionary in Malawi, and as someone committed to social justice and political activism, he had become involved in a movement to resist what many perceived to be the repressive policies of the country's new president, Hastings Banda. He was abruptly deported from Malawi and returned to Scotland. In his lectures on the history of Christian missions, he would say that of course Christianity came to Africa along with empire. 'Christianity, Commerce and Civilization', as David Livingstone famously put it. The arrival of Christianity also heralded the arrival of oppressive colonisation and exploitation. The missionaries who often proclaimed themselves as Moses, leading people to a new and promised land, were more akin, in reality, to Pharaoh, subjecting people to slavery rather than liberating them. But, argued Ross, contained within the texts that the missionaries brought was a subversive story of a profound reversal. For the Gospel provided for the new subjects of the British Empire a manifesto for their liberation from the yoke of oppression. The way of Jesus, which is the way of weakness, powerlessness and resistance has, at its heart, a message that the way of self-emptying is also the way to win new life, to find a pathway to justice and to enable people and communities genuinely to flourish.

How do we square the image of the gentle suffering Christ with the strident, intolerant messages of the 'Killing Time' of the 1680s, during which thousands were persecuted and died in Scotland on all sides of a religious divide. For some, the struggle was in the name of establishing what Knox described as 'the Godly Commonwealth' whilst for others it was ensuring that the king could control the powerful church through the appointment of bishops. The exercise of such power, from whatever side, always produces its innocent victims. In the modern world it is sadly the case that some of the most damaged people you'll ever meet are people who have been negatively treated in the name of religion.

What I encountered again and again on the Camino is what I encounter elsewhere in our society — a changing culture, a shift in self-identity and a refusal to be shoe-horned into compliance with a rigid belief system. People no longer identify themselves in the narrow ways of even a generation ago. They live and work internationally. They marry internationally, they marry partners of the same sex, if indeed they marry at all. Our society has become pluralist and multicultural. Gender identity has changed, and for so many people it feels as though some of the attitudes of entities like the church are light-years behind the rest of society. Many people no longer define themselves in terms of a specific faith community, but that does not mean that they are devoid of faith or a spirituality that is open to the possibilities of mystery. For growing numbers of people the former tribal identities of race, religion and nation no longer make sense. Nor do the constraints of dogma, which are increasingly seen for what they are – not propositions about truth, but instruments of control and coercion. Many of us grew up with the threat of hell and damnation looming over us, even in the middle years of the twentieth century.

Historically, the Christian church began life as a persecuted minority. Merely to profess faith in Jesus was to run the risk of being killed or imprisoned, and certainly, the 'People of the Way', as the first Christians were known, had little, if any, power within society. Then, in a remarkable turn in fortunes, the Roman Emperor Constantine embraced Christianity following the battle of Milvian Bridge in AD 312, when, it is believed, Christian symbols painted on the shields of Constantine's soldiers gave them victory. Whatever the truth of that story, Christianity adopted the clothes of empire and became an institution that, in its various forms, has wielded colossal power throughout the last 1,600 years. Rather than dressing in the simple dress of a Galilean peasant, as Jesus did, the church has dressed itself in emblems of privilege and status.

But there is something changing in the church, and the idea of the 'Christian empire' seems to be disappearing into the sand. The church is, in these times, having to redefine the manner of its presence in the world. Perhaps the most significant pioneer of this new form of ministry is the person who sits on the last vestige of the Christian empire, the papal throne of Rome, Pope Francis. He has set out an agenda of humility, openness and service for the church that some of his cardinals and other officials find very challenging. I have a friend who teaches ecclesiastical history and spends a good deal of time in the Vatican library. He says that Pope Francis can regularly be seen queuing up for lunch in the Vatican canteen with the rest of those working there.

Just as Jesus removed his outer garment and thereby removed his robe of office, as it were, and, putting a towel round himself, washed his disciples' feet, so the church is in these times rediscovering humility, a servant model of ministry. Success is not a Christian word; whether that means shows of power or numerical strength, success is not, nor probably ever should have been, the measure of the impact of the Christian message on the world. The Kingdom of God is at hand. It is very near you, as someone once said. It is so near at hand it sometimes takes you by the hand. It is there alongside the poor, the lame, the lost, the forsaken, the downtrodden and all those who long for deeper 'aliveness' and joy. That's what worship points to. Christ's Kingdom offers an alternative imagination that does not conform to the patterns of this passing world; it conforms to a pattern that puts mercy and humility in charge.

The Christian church is going through a period of upheaval, just as it did 500 years ago when Martin Luther began a process that changed the world. Some characterise this not so much as a period of reform as a period of decline into obscurity and ultimately oblivion. I am not so sure.

I began this account of my journey to Santiago with the story of how I discovered my fragility and vulnerability. I had begun full of self-reliant vigour. I had been in a defiant, competitive mood, eager to get ahead, to win a race, to show others how fit I was. After three days I found myself helpless and grateful for the ministry of Jacques, who came to my rescue unbidden, a kindly stranger. He asked for no reward. There was no transaction in our encounter; love was not the subject of a bargain. Instead, it had its own overflowing currency that surprised us both because it could not be spent. Rather, it became its own multiplier as he enabled me to minister to him, in return, in the morning.

There is no limit, no boundary, no vocabulary of ideas that you can construct that will ever tame the wild goose of the Spirit. This love, this message, is utterly free and unbound. That is what people sense and search for on the pilgrim way to Santiago. That is the way the world so desperately needs to find and follow.

We need to be liberated from the tragedies of plunder, greed, division and prejudice that have often emerged out of religion and have left their mark on our societies and on our fragile planet. It was Tony Benn, I think, who once said that faith is something that people die for whilst doctrine is something people kill for. Faith is about a relationship of trust, not a sword-wielding certainty like Santiago, Mata Moros – 'St James the Moor-slayer', whom I encountered in the Benedictine monastery at Samos.

One day, in the British Museum, Kate and I came across an arresting short poem called 'Choose' by Carl Sandburg:

The single clenched fist, lifted and ready,
Or the open, asking hand, held out and waiting.
Choose:
For we meet by one or the other.

Along the pilgrim way I met so many people with open, asking hands held out in friendship, eager to build communities of inclusion and understanding. Many of the stories we read about in church are about Jesus helping those who struggle, speaking up for justice, showing compassion and building a caring community in which people are not harshly judged. The challenge is to put those ideals into practice in our daily lives and build hope-filled, flourishing local communities in a world that makes room for the rest of creation too.

All of this points to the need for something very old to be found anew: a community of those who don't judge others or cling to power, privilege and position, but in humility offer hospitality and discover the miracle of the empty-handed stranger as the bearer of the most treasured gifts.

I think of Myron, the friend I made on that hot day back in La Rioja. This good and kindly man, hounded and persecuted by the rulers of his church, was now set free to minister with a generous open heart in his coffee shop. One day I'd like to visit, and I am certain that the atmosphere of his coffee house will have more of a feel of church than the congregation he ministered to and who chewed him up and spat him out. Probably, Myron's coffee house is the sort of place Jesus might frequent with his friends rather than an ecclesiastical monument like the cathedral at Burgos, overpowered as it is by the gold and show that celebrates the plunder of the new world by the Conquistadores and the ethnic cleansing accomplished by El Cid.

If the Camino has taught me anything, it has reinforced my commitment to working to build communities of trust and friendship which are free of prejudice and the abuse of power, where people seek out the essential goodness and grace that is at the heart of all. To allow ourselves to be vulnerable and to be helped by strangers can be hard, and goes against the grain of self-reliance. But if we ask for help when things go wrong, if we accept that we all have times of vulnerability, far from being diminished, we will discover the richness of a caring community that grows through kindness. We must recognise that we are not fully our own, and that whatever the mystery that the church is, the best of it is not the fallible, human institution it has so often become but a mysterious initiative we do not control which will surprise us and often take our breath away. We should anticipate gifts, rather than thinking we only have gifts to give, and realise that there is inexhaustible goodness and inspiration out there waiting to lift us up. We must overcome gender stereotypes and find that gender justice is a means of peacemaking in our own homes and communities.

All this I have learned, discovered and experienced between Le Puy-en-Velay and Santiago de Compostela. I'm grateful to the Camino; it represents that thing we start out 'to do' but which takes hold and 'does' us.

ACKNOWLEDGEMENTS

An encounter by a hospital bed with Bill Cameron inspired my first pilgrimage walk from Iona to Old Aberdeen 20 years ago. I am grateful to Bill and Peter Stephen, my first pilgrimage companions, to Jon and Jo, who joined me on the Camino, and to Mary for the stick! I'm also grateful to the late Andrew Patterson, whose passion for pilgrimage and ecology inspired me whilst we were wayward students together at New College, holding our 'alternative' seminars in the Jolly Judge.

I want to say thank you to Ann Crawford, who found me and helped me believe that writing is something I should try. The wonderful team at Birlinn are so professional and supportive and such fun to work with – thanks to them all. Thanks also to Alastair McIntosh and Ricky Ross for their kind words. Family and friends have given helpful comments along the way, especially Judith Smith, who read the first drafts eagerly and wanted more.

I'd like to dedicate this book to my wife, Kate and our children, Will, Jay and Tom. We are on a wonderful pilgrimage together, and I thank you all for your wisdom, laughter and love. And, finally, a big thank you to the congregation of Greyfriars Kirk, Edinburgh, who've encouraged, befriended and tolerated me for so many happy years and sent me off to Santiago as a way of celebrating a quarter of a century of ministry.

Richard Frazer
March 2019

BIBLIOGRAPHY

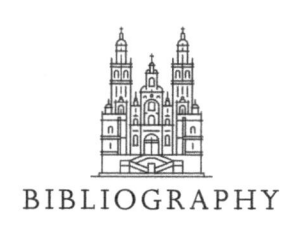

Brierley, John, *A Pilgrim's Guide to the Camino de Santiago — a Practical and Mystical Manual for the Modern Day Pilgrim*, Findhorn Press, 2012

The British Pilgrimage Trust website www.britishpilgrimage.org

Chatwin, Bruce, *The Songlines*, Penguin, 1988

Chaucer, Geoffrey, *The Canterbury Tales*, trans. Nevill Coghill, Penguin Classics, 1988

Clouteau, Lauriane and Jacques Clouteau, *Miam Miam Dodo: Chemin de Compostelle*, Les Editions du Vieux Crayon, 2012

Dillard, Annie, *For the Time Being*, Vintage, 1999

Dillard, Annie, *Pilgrim at Tinker Creek*, Harper Perennial Modern Classics, 1999

Duffy, Eamon, *Saints and Sinners: A History of the Popes*, Yale University Press, 1997

Gibbon, Edward, *The History of the Decline and Fall of the Roman Empire*, ed. David Womersley, Penguin Classics, 2000

Gros, Frédéric, *A History of Walking*, Verso, 2015

Guinness, Alec, *My Name Escapes Me*, Penguin Books, 1996

Hammer, Joshua, 'Is a lack of water to blame for the conflict in Syria?, *Smithsonian Magazine*, June 2013

Lewis, C.S., *The Four Loves*, Harcourt Books, 1960

Luther, Martin, *Luther's Works*, Table Talk: Volume 54, Fortress Press, 1967

Macfarlane, Robert, 'Rites of way: behind the pilgrimage revival', *The Guardian*, 15 June 2012

Mackinnon, Donald, *The Stripping of the Altars*, Fontana Books, 1969

Massingham, H.J., *The Tree of Life*, Jon Carpenter Publishing, 2004

McLaren, Brian, *The Great Spiritual Migration*, Hodder and Stoughton, 2016

Miller, John, *A Simple Life, Roland Walls and the Community of the Transfiguration*, St Andrew Press, 2014

Muir, Edwin, *An Autobiography*, Canongate Classics, 1993

Robb, Graham, *The Discovery of France*, Picador, 2016

Sandburg, Carl, *Chicago Poems*, Henry Holt and Company, 1916

Shepherd, Nan, *The Living Mountain*, Canongate Books, 2011

Sherrard, Philip, *The Eclipse of Man and Nature*, Golgonooza Press, 1987

Solzhenitsyn, Aleksandr, *The Gulag Archipelago: 1918–56*, Harvill Press Editions, 2003

Smith, Adam, *The Wealth of Nations*, Capstone Classics, 2010

Stevenson, Robert Louis, *Travels with a Donkey*, Collins, 1910